A Public God

A Public God

Natural Theology Reconsidered

Neil Ormerod

Fortress Press
Minneapolis

A PUBLIC GOD
Natural Theology Reconsidered

Cover image: © Thinkstock. Grunge background/Zonnar_RF/Thinkstock
Cover design: Alisha Lofgren

Library of Congress Cataloging-in-Publication Data
Print ISBN: 978-1-4514-6469-6
eBook ISBN: 978-1-4514-6983-7

The paper used in this publication meets the minimum requirements of
American National Standard for Information Sciences — Permanence of Paper
for Printed Library Materials, ANSI Z329.48-1984.

Manufactured in the U.S

This book was produced using PressBooks.com, and PDF rendering was done by
PrinceXML.

Contents

Preface

The purpose of this book is to act as a companion piece for the work I wrote with my friend and colleague Cynthia Crysdale, *Creator God, Evolving World*.[1] That book operated largely with a framework of a natural theology to argue that the classical conception of God—as all knowing, all powerful, and unchanging—is perfectly adequate to deal with the new world of scientific discoveries, such as evolution and quantum mechanics, that are often seen as either rendering God irrelevant or as requiring some fundamental rethinking of the divine nature. In that sense, it was a defense of classical theism. However, in that work we did not address directly the question of God's existence. That God exists was more or less presupposed, though we noted some directions that give an indication as to why one might want to affirm God's existence.

This book, by contrast, is a work in natural theology that seeks to address the question of God's existence. Nonetheless, it does not simply seek to spell out various proofs for God's existence and discuss their strengths and weaknesses. It attempts to go a bit deeper, to ask about what sorts of cultural shifts we currently face that render arguments for God's existence so problematic, and how these shifts

---

1. Neil Ormerod and Cynthia S. W. Crysdale, *Creator God, Evolving World* (Minneapolis: Fortress Press, 2013).

might be addressed. In that sense, it seeks to reformulate natural theology as a culturally *contextual theology* rather than some philosophical decontextualized argument. At present, that context is dominated by the writings of the so-called new atheists—Richard Dawkins, Christopher Hitchens and others—who draw on sciences, politics and "reason" to dismiss belief in God and religions that support this belief.

This work also aims to see natural theology as a form of *public theology*. Much is written today about the need to bring theological resources to bear in discussing matters of public interest and concern, such as the impact of globalization, secularization in the West, or the debates surrounding religion and science. Many of these attempts, fine works in themselves, still draw on explicit elements of a particular religious tradition, rendering them less accessible to those outside that tradition. While this present work sits firmly within the Christian tradition in that it draws on well-worn paths present in the history of Christian thought on natural theology, nonetheless it prescinds from explicitly Christian beliefs or the use of Christian authors as "authorities" to settle arguments. The arguments need to stand or fall in their own right. However, to do so it must examine and challenge the notions of public reason that operate in our context, seeking alternatives that are more conducive to religious belief (see chapter 2).

Finally, natural theology is not just contextual and public, but also a form of *political theology*. Political theology is concerned with the political consequences of religious belief in terms of policies on matters such as economics, migration, gender issues, and bioethics. Often, such theologies will seek to draw direct political consequences from specific religious commitments, an approach that raises questions about the interrelationship of faith and politics, church and state. Such incursions into politics often run counter to the ethos of separation of church and state and the aggressive secularism present in the West. In dealing with these matters, we often seem to find ourselves caught between either the complete elimination of religion from political debates or a return to a theocratic Christendom (or its Islamic equivalent).

However, a successful natural theology presents a God who is known through a form of publicly accessible reason. Such a stance calls into question the process of radical secularization that effectively marginalizes religions and rules out political appeals to God. As a form of political theology, natural theology must consider the political consequences of the public acknowledgment of God's existence. It must face the false dichotomy of either secularization or theocracy head-on, to suggest ways in which there can be public acknowledgment of God's existence without the consequence of theocracy or a return to Christendom. The proposal developed in chapter 6 is tentative, but it does suggest that the current dichotomy does not exhaust all possible alternatives.

The key issue that emerges in the book is what Bernard Lonergan calls "intellectual conversion" (and, to a lesser extent, "moral conversion"). Such a conversion requires a shift in our unreflective stances on the meaning of terms like "reality" and "existence." In his major work, *Insight,* Lonergan speaks of two forms of knowing: one based on human reasoning, the other on animal extroversion.[2] What he means by "intellectual conversion" is learning to distinguish these two forms of knowing and committing oneself to a fully human knowing based on reasoning, including the metaphysical implications this has for our notion of reality.[3] It has become

---

2. Bernard J. F. Lonergan, *Insight: A Study of Human Understanding*, ed. Frederick E. Crowe and Robert M. Doran, vol. 3, Collected Works of Bernard Lonergan (Toronto: University of Toronto Press, 1992), 11–12.

3. While Lonergan does not use the term "intellectual conversion" in *Insight*, it is basic to the program of self-appropriation present in the book. The terminology derives from his later writings.

increasingly clear to me that without something like intellectual conversion, any argument for the existence of God will remain "unreal." As will be shown in the current work, the general lack of such conversion, evident across the board among scientists and many philosophers, gives some idea of the cultural difficulty to be faced. Such a process of conversion is not alien to the scientific method. Nonetheless, it runs against the grain of the implicit philosophical stance of many of the new atheists, with their appeals to the findings of science (chapter 3). Nonetheless, such a conversion is startlingly strange when first encountered, and must overcome the persistent myth that somehow reality is limited to what we see!

While the work with Cynthia provided the motivation for the present work, it did not emerge without other precursors. I have written a number of research papers that address the question of natural theology in various ways, as well as some more popular pieces that have appeared on the Australian Broadcasting Commission Religion and Ethics website.[4] The present work is not simply a repeat of these, but a major reordering of the material with substantial new material as well. I hope it offers a more coherent account than the more occasional pieces have allowed. I should also note that I have not repeated material found in my book with Cynthia. That book more than adequately deals with a number of objections raised by atheists, particularly the objection that evolution and other chance processes rule out the possibility of divine design. Interested readers should refer to that work if this is the question they are seeking to address.

4. The academic pieces include Neil Ormerod, "God and Politics," *Australasian Catholic Record* 84 (2007); Ormerod, "In Defence of Natural Theology: Bringing God into the Public Realm," *Irish Theological Quarterly* 71 (2007); Ormerod, "Charles Taylor and Bernard Lonergan on Natural Theology," *Irish Theological Quarterly* 74 (2009); Ormerod, "Preliminary Steps Towards a Natural Theology," *Irish Theological Quarterly* 76 (2011); Ormerod, "Secularisation and the 'Rise' of Atheism," *Australian EJournal of Theology* 17 (2010). The ABC website for Religion and Ethics is http://www.abc.net.au/religion/.

In bringing this work to completion, I would like to thank various people for their assistance and encouragement, particularly my friends and colleagues Cynthia Crysdale and Shane Clifton, with whom I had many fruitful conversations, and from whom I received helpful feedback on the text. I would also like to thank my graduate students John Collins, Dominic Arcamone, and David Perry for their feedback on the text. Much of this work was completed while I enjoyed hospitality at three institutions, the University of San Diego with Professor Gerard Mannion, Sewanee University of the South with Professor Cynthia Crysdale, and Marquette University with Professor Robert Doran, SJ, during my sabbatical leave in 2012. I am very grateful to each for the overwhelming generosity they showed me. Finally I would like to thank the staff at Fortress Press, particularly Michael Gibson, for their commitment to theological publishing and their willingness to take up this particular project.

1

Natural Theology as Contextual, Political, and Public

At its most basic, natural theology is about the "God question," that is, the question of the existence and attributes of a presumed divine being. As a "natural" theology, it does not seek to draw upon any particular religious tradition or revelation (which, after all, would be circular), but rather works from some account of human reasoning, with a degree of public accountability, in dialogue with the other products of (nonreligious) human reasoning. While I am a Christian and Catholic theologian, this is not a work in Christian or Catholic theology per se, though it does rework themes drawn from within the Christian tradition. Nor is it a theology of "nature" or the "natural world." Though it is interested in what science tells us about the natural world, it is as interested in what the very activity of science itself tells us about the nature of human intelligence and reason that drive science, and the implications this activity has about reality.

These are some of the resources that a "natural" theology will draw upon in addressing the God question.

Still, a question is never an abstraction; it arises in a context. The context of the God question today is very different from that of many of the great figures—such as Plato, Aristotle, and Aquinas—who have sought to address it in the past. Nor is it just an intellectual question, a matter of mere curiosity for the idle minds of philosophers and theologians. It is an existential and indeed a political question with profound personal and social consequences. Western societies have undergone a progressive secularization, the increasing exclusion of religion from the public square. Some of this exclusion has been pragmatic, carving out a space free from religious disputation to allow for social harmony among competing religious claims. Some has been ideological, driven by a desire to limit religion to the private sphere, to make of religious belief a purely internal commitment with no possibility of extending its claims into a public arena dominated by reason alone. The public claims of reason are then to be contrasted with the private, and possibly irrational (or at best a-rational), beliefs of religious traditions.

This context has taken on a sharper edge with the emergence of the so-called new atheism, steered by the leading lights of Richard Dawkins and Christopher Hitchens.[1] This new breed of atheists has taken atheism out of the confines of academic philosophical debates and onto the streets, holding international atheist conventions that attract people from around the world in a global "celebration of reason."[2] This movement is not concerned with polite intellectual disagreement, but more with street brawling or trench warfare, as anyone who has entered the world of online publishing and blogging

1. Richard Dawkins, *The God Delusion* (London: Bantam, 2006); Christopher Hitchens, *God Is Not Great: How Religion Poisons Everything*, 1st ed. (New York: Twelve, 2007)
2. Two such international conventions have been held in Melbourne Australia, in 2011 and 2012. Richard Dawkins was a keynote speaker at both.

can attest.[3] Online, the gloves are off and religious positions and beliefs are mercilessly pilloried as ignorant, irrational, unscientific, and dangerous. As the not-so-subtle subtitle of Hitchens book suggests, "Religion poisons *everything*."

It seems clear that the background to this overt display of anger is public perception of the rise of militant Islam.[4] While hardly representative of Islam more broadly, this movement, especially in light of the terrorist acts of 9/11, has significantly raised the temperature surrounding the God question. Islamic belief stands in some tension with the assumptions present in the secularizing West; in Islam, religious belief is expected to be expressed in appropriate dress codes and public actions. Islam has its own legal and economic traditions, which may be in conflict with legal and economic traditions in the West. In some ways, Islam raises the specter of a history that the West has rejected, not without good reason, of basing a society on religious beliefs. The prospect of an "Islamic state" recalls the ghosts of Christendom in the West and becomes a looming threat of a renewed theocracy. In such a context, the status of natural theology as a form of political theology becomes more evident. If God's existence is viewed as not only compatible with reason, but as even mandated by reason, where does that leave the agenda of secularization? And what alternatives can one envisage to Christendom or Islamic theocracy if God's existence is acknowledged in the public realm?

There is a broader cultural context, which has been mapped out in some detail in the work of Charles Taylor. Taylor begins his book

---

3. See Alister E. McGrath, *Why God Won't Go Away: Is the New Atheism Running on Empty?* (Nashville: Thomas Nelson, 2010) for an account of this online world of atheism.

4. For example, in a 2003 interview, "Hitchens said that the events of September 11th filled him with 'exhilaration.'" See Ian Parker "He Knew He Was Right: How a former socialist became the Iraq war's fiercest defender," *The New Yorker* (October 16, 2006), available at http://www.newyorker.com/archive/2006/10/16/061016fa_fact_parker?currentPage=all.

A Secular Age with a carefully nuanced account of secularization, distinguishing three distinct meanings that can be given to the term: secularization as (1) the withdrawal of God from "public spaces," for example through the separation of church and state; (2) a decline in religious practice; and (3) "a move from a society where belief in God is unchallenged and indeed, unproblematic, to one in which it is understood to be one option among others, and frequently not the easiest to embrace."[5] As Taylor notes, a society can be secular in the sense of (1) but still have relatively high rates of religious practice, as for example in the United States, and so not display secularization in the sense of (2). However, what is of most concern for his analysis is the third sense: "The change I want to define and trace is one which takes us from a society in which it was virtually impossible not to believe in God, to one in which faith, even for the staunchest believer, is one possibility among others. . . . Belief in God is no longer axiomatic. There are alternatives."[6]

The third sense is the one of most interest to the project of natural theology: this movement from a world where the existence of God was taken for granted to a world where it is just one possibility among others, and not necessarily the easiest stance to maintain intellectually. For Taylor, the most significant factor in this shift is not the rise of modern science, contra the claims of many of the new atheists, but the movement to what he calls an "immanent frame," marked by a turn away from the outer world, leading to a growth in the vocabulary of interiority, of thought and feeling.[7] The emergence of an immanent frame drives "a new form of religious life, more personal, committed, devoted,"[8] but it also creates a new

5. Charles Taylor, *A Secular Age* (Cambridge, MA: Belknap, 2007), 3.
6. Ibid., 3.
7. Ibid., 539. Taylor's account here has similarities with Lonergan's notion of the "turn to the subject" and the emergence of a "third stage of meaning" grounded in human interiority.
8. Ibid., 541.

distinction: "This frame constitutes a 'natural' order, to be contrasted to a 'supernatural' one, an 'immanent' world, over against a possible 'transcendent one.'"[9] This leads to the construction of a "closed world view" that methodologically excludes reference to the transcendent. While Taylor does not think that this is a necessary outcome of the emergence of the immanent frame, he does acknowledge that within such a worldview "the inference to the transcendent is at the extreme and most fragile end of a chain of inferences; it is the most epistemically questionable."[10]

These are the challenges to be raised and faced in this book. It is not simply a work *in* natural theology so much as it is a work *about* natural theology and how it is to be conceived. Underlying it is the proposal that we reconceive of natural theology as contextual, public, and political—not as an exercise in intellectual gymnastics seeking to infer God's existence "at the extreme and most fragile end of a chain of inferences," but as a process where the very engagement is as important as the conclusions reached. As *contextual*, natural theology must recognize the intellectual context of its engagement against a background of broad cultural shifts of the type Taylor has identified. The context of Aquinas's "five ways" is not the context of twenty-first-century Western culture. For one thing, the ability to recognize metaphysics as a distinct form of reasoning has all but vanished in our time, and we barely recognize the loss. As *public*, natural theology must grapple with the God question in ways that prescind from the particular faith commitments of our competing religious traditions and present the case for God in a way that is accessible to

---

9. Ibid., 542. It is worth noting that Taylor's use of the term *supernatural* here is conditioned by the emergence of the immanent frame. If the immanent frame prescribes the limits of the "natural," then knowledge of God's existence is necessarily supernatural in the sense of being beyond nature. Then natural theology becomes impossible. However, as Taylor notes, this construction of the immanent frame is only a "spin," not a necessary outcome of the move to the subject.
10. Ibid., 558.

public reason. Still, this might mean combating hegemonic claims, particularly those that would suggest that scientific reason is the only valid form of public reasoning. Finally, as *political*, natural theology has to explore the political implications of what it might mean for God's existence to be a publicly acknowledged fact, not avoiding concerns about theocracy or a new Christendom but arguing that public acknowledgment of God does not necessarily lead us down that road.

However, before undertaking this more extended project, we should get our bearings by considering some of the history and contexts of previous exercises in and debates about natural theology.

The Beginnings of Natural Theology

We can trace the beginnings of natural theology in the West to the emergence of philosophy in ancient Greece. The Greek discovery of mind and its potentialities had a profound impact on Western culture, but it was not a discovery that went without mishap. Socrates's persistent questioning of the Athenians brought about his demise, charged with corrupting the youth and disputing the existence of the gods. This is not to say that he did not believe in the existence of *a* God. Indeed, he developed a teleological argument, or argument from design, to seek to prove the existence of God. However, he did provide a solid philosophical critique of the religious beliefs of his day, seeking to eliminate their mythological aspects. Plato continued this approach, conceiving of a highest good that was the goal or purpose of human living. However, it is Plato's pupil Aristotle who is most famous for conceiving of God as an "unmoved mover," whose existence can explain all movement in the cosmos.[11]

---

11. Aristotle, *Physics*, Book 8, 259a, in Aristotle, *The Basic Works of Aristotle*, ed. Richard McKeon, Modern Library Classics (New York: Random House, 2009), 374–75.

It is important to note that these arguments toward the existence of God did not occur in the face of skepticism about belief in divine beings. Indeed, the Greek pantheon was full of gods and goddesses whose worship was an accepted aspect of the social order and whose capriciousness was mirrored by the leaders of Greek society. Cosmos and polis ran parallel to one another, ruled by passion and torn by conflict, the realm of the gods reflecting that of the social order. The discovery of mind by these ancient philosophers suggested a radically new principle for ordering society: an ordering according to the dictates of reason. And so both Plato and Aristotle produced new political visions and ethical reflections to guide human living. Within these reflections, God is not an extraneous addition but the principle that holds the whole together, the one whose existence makes sense of the rest of the structure.

Christianity would later take up some interest in questions of natural theology, reflecting in general on the apostle Paul's comments about the "pagans" in Rom. 1:19-20:

> For what can be known about God is plain to them, because God has shown it to them. Ever since the creation of the world his eternal power and divine nature, invisible though they are, have been understood and seen through the things he has made.

However, it was not until the Middle Ages and the emergence of Scholasticism that the question took on a new energy. Again, the context is significant: there was a rediscovery of the works of Aristotle, through the mediation of Islamic scholars; new educational institutions, universities, were founded in Paris and Bologna; and there was a renewed confidence in the abilities of reason to know the world apart from the dictates of religious tradition. As with the era of the Greek philosophers, it was not a time of skepticism about the existence of God. Indeed, it was a highly religious era where the Christian Church dominated social and cultural life. However, the new emphasis on reason raised questions about the relationship between God and the world. Does reason lead us to God, or away from God? Is reason a distinct source of authority from God, or does its authority derive from and serve divine authority? Aquinas's "five ways," perhaps the most famous contribution to natural theology in history, find their context in such questions. Not only does reason lead us to the existence of God, but human reason is a created participation in the divine reason, and so subservient to it. Faith and reason are harmonious allies in the pursuit of a genuinely religious life. We shall return to the issue of Aquinas's context in the next chapter.

Growing Skepticism about Reason

This synthesis between faith and reason was not to last. Late Scholastic emphasis on so-called universal concepts led to an increasing skepticism about the powers of reason, resulting in a widespread nominalism—the belief that the intellect only knows the names of things, not the things themselves. This philosophical skepticism bled over into the religious realm during the Reformation, leading to the rejection of the earlier project of natural theology. Luther was not taken so much with Rom. 1:19-20 as he was with Rom. 1:21: "for though they knew God, they did not honor him as God or give thanks to him, but they became futile in their thinking, and their senseless minds were darkened." The darkening of the mind due to the impact of original sin meant that reason could not be trusted to arrive at knowledge of the one true God. On this antinomy of faith and reason Luther proclaimed:

> There is on earth among all dangers no more dangerous thing than a
> richly endowed and adroit reason, especially if she enters into spiritual

matters which concern the soul and God. . . . Reason must be . . . blinded, and destroyed. Faith must trample underfoot all reason, sense, and understanding, and whatever it sees it must put out of sight. . . . Whoever wants to be a Christian should tear the eyes out of his reason.[12]

Reason had become a seducer that would lead Christians into apostasy and heresy. Again, such a stance was not without its own context. The Catholic Church of the time had embraced all the excesses of the renewed humanism of the Renaissance and was wallowing in ecclesiastical corruption. If this is where a synthesis of faith and reason was to lead believers, one can understand why Luther might want to reject it.

This separation of faith and reason was to be given philosophical legitimacy by the work of Immanuel Kant. Spurred by the growing skepticism about the powers of reason articulated by the empiricist philosopher David Hume,[13] Kant developed an elaborate philosophical response that sought to give legitimacy to speculative or "pure" reason in relation to the empirical world of science, while robbing it of legitimacy in relation to metaphysical questions such as the existence of God. He distinguished between *phenomena* (things-for-us) and *noumena* (things-in-themselves), arguing that while the mind can know *phenomena*, this being the basis for scientific discovery, *noumena* remained beyond the reach of reason. Kant effectively ruled metaphysics out of court, limiting human reason to the phenomenal world of sense:

---

12. Quoted in Walter Kaufmann, *The Faith of a Heretic* (Garden City, NY: Doubleday, 1963), 75. Ironically, this quote is regularly referred to on atheist websites and can even be purchased emblazoned on a T-shirt.

13. David Hume was a Scottish Enlightenment philosopher and a key figure in British empiricism. His skepticism about knowledge led him to deny any grasp of causality. More famously, he argued against the credibility of any account of miracles. Kant claims that reading Hume awoke him from his "dogmatic slumber," leading him to rethink his own position on cognition and metaphysics.

The light dove cleaving in free flight the thin air, whose resistance it feels, might imagine that her movements would be far more free and rapid in airless space. Just in the same way did Plato, abandoning the world of sense because of the narrow limits it sets to the understanding, venture upon the wings of ideas beyond it, into the void space of pure intellect. He did not reflect that he made no real progress by all his efforts; for he met with no resistance which might serve him for a support, as it were, whereon to rest, and on which he might apply his powers, in order to let the intellect acquire momentum for its progress.[14]

In particular, Kant declared three metaphysical truths to be beyond pure reason: the existence of God; the immortality of the soul; and the freedom of the will. He did argue, however, that these three truths were essential to practical reason, and that a reasoned ethics was impossible without them.

Kant was responding not just to Hume but to the growing success of the natural sciences in providing an explanatory account of the world. Isaac Newton and his successors had unraveled the secrets of planetary motion, solving problems that had puzzled humanity for millennia. Still, Newton conceived of his work as one of "natural philosophy," raising the question of whether and how science, properly so-called, was distinct from metaphysics. Kant had provided the basis for such a distinction with the categories of phenomena and noumena, which sought to provide a philosophical grounding for the sciences while eliminating the possibility of metaphysics. Reason was indeed successful, but only in the scientific realm, not in the realm of things divine or metaphysical. Meanwhile, Kant's ethics seemed to have a foot in both camps, seeking to be derived from practical reason alone, while evoking the above three principles from beyond pure reason as its basic requirements.

14. Immanuel Kant, *The Critique of Pure Reason*, trans. Norman Kemp Smith (New York: St. Martin's Press, 1929, 1965), 48.

Of course, Kant would never deny the existence of God, just the validity of seeking to prove God's existence. One of his major works was his *Religion within the Boundaries of Mere Reason*.[15] Whereas Luther sought to pit faith against reason to promote faith, the outcome of Kant's philosophy was to pit reason against faith, or at least the claims of revealed religion. All the religious truth we need is accessible to practical reason, and if it is not accessible, it is not important. Supernatural elements were not essential to his notion of religion unless they could be derived from the demands of practical reason, and so, for example, Kant saw no practical consequences to belief in the Trinity.[16] Revealed religion did not enjoy the universality of reason that everyone possessed. Kant challenged his readers to "dare to think" without reliance on traditional authorities.[17]

Kant's work was enormously influential and remains an important backdrop to contemporary debates. In his work, we find questions that continue to be raised in debates between believers and atheists: the significance of the rise of modern science for religious belief; the possibility of distinguishing between science and metaphysics, indeed the very possibility of metaphysics distinct from science; and the relationship between reason, religion, and ethical reasoning. In one way or another, these questions continue to inhabit contemporary discussions on God, science, and morality.

---

15. Immanuel Kant, *Religion within the Boundaries of Mere Reason and Other Writings*, ed. Allen Wood, George Di Giovanni, and Robert Merrihew Adams, Cambridge Texts in the History of Philosophy (Cambridge/New York: Cambridge University Press, 1998).
16. Ibid., 143.
17. In fact Kant's appeal to practical reason managed to incorporate many elements of Lutheran theology, such as doctrines of original sin, the *simul justus et peccator*, and imputed righteousness.

A Catholic Response at Vatican I

Kant's philosophy cemented the faith-reason antinomy that emerged during the Reformation. Indeed, the teachings of Vatican I on the question of faith and reason are framed by the contexts of Luther and Kant. At the time there were, on the one hand, the Catholic traditionalists who, like Luther, sought to draw a line between faith and reason; on the other hand were the rationalists who, like Kant, thought that all religious truth should be accessible by reason alone.

In response, the council reaffirmed the inner unity of faith and reason, both of which have their source in the one God: "It is the same God who reveals the mysteries and infuses faith, and who has endowed the human mind with the light of reason."[18] Against the rationalists, it maintained that there are some truths revealed by God that remain inaccessible to reason: "There are proposed for our belief mysteries hidden in God which, unless they are divinely revealed, are incapable of being known." Perhaps primary among these are the mysteries of the Trinity and the Incarnation. Against the traditionalists, it affirmed the power of reason to know certain things without the need for revelation. This included things such as the moral law, though the moral teaching contained in revelation assists our reason, weakened because of the impact of sin, to arrive at moral truth.

But perhaps of greater interest in the context of a natural theology, the council taught:

> The same Holy mother Church holds and teaches that God, the source and end of all things, can be known with certainty from the consideration of created things, by the natural power of human reason: ever since the creation of the world, his invisible nature has been clearly perceived in the things that have been made.

18. For this and the following quotes from Vatican I, see the dogmatic decree *De Filius*, available at http://www.ewtn.com/library/councils/v1.htm.

This teaching was then reinforced by the following condemnation: "If anyone says that the one, true God, our creator and lord, cannot be known with certainty from the things that have been made, by the natural light of human reason: let him be anathema." This same positive teaching (as distinct from the anathema) is repeated verbatim in the Dogmatic Constitution on Divine Revelation, *Dei Verbum*, of the Second Vatican Council.[19]

The key word in the teaching of the Councils is "natural."[20] During the debate at Vatican I, the word "natural" was inserted to distinguish what was being stated from any claim that could be made about "fallen reason." According to the standard Catholic theology of the day, original sin weakens the will in pursuit of the good and darkens the mind in pursuit of the true. Vatican I thus makes no claim about the status of fallen reason's ability to know God's existence.[21] The point of difference between the Catholic position and Luther's position regarding the powers of reason might then revolve around differing accounts of the role of grace and its healing effects, both on the will and the intellect. The Catholic theology of grace allows for reason to have its powers restored and strengthened, and so Catholic theologian Bernard Lonergan can paradoxically conclude an essay on the possibility of natural knowledge of God with the following: "I do not think that in this life people arrive at natural knowledge of God without God's grace, but what I do not doubt is that the knowledge they so attain is natural."[22]

---

19. See *Dei Verbum*, n. 6, available at http://www.vatican.va/archive/hist_councils/ii_vatican_council/documents/vat-ii_const_19651118_dei-verbum_en.html.
20. However, I would note as an aside that the word "natural" is missing in the English translation of *Dei Verbum*, but present in the other translations on the Vatican web site.
21. For an account of the debate at the Council and the meaning of its teaching, see Fergus Kerr, "Knowing God by Reason Alone: What Vatican I Never Said," *New Blackfriars* (2010): 215–28.
22. Bernard J. F. Lonergan, "Natural Knowledge of God," in *A Second Collection*, ed. William Ryan and Bernard Tyrrell (Philadelphia: Westminster, 1974), 133.

Vatican I went on to express the harmony of faith and reason in the following terms: "Even though faith is above reason, there can never be any real disagreement between faith and reason, since it is the same God who reveals the mysteries and infuses faith, and who has endowed the human mind with the light of reason." Clearly in mind here are the then-recent developments in science, particularly Darwin's teaching on biological evolution. While a note of caution is evident—"all faithful Christians are forbidden to defend as the legitimate conclusions of science those opinions which are known to be contrary to the doctrine of faith"—the solution is not the rejection of science. Rather, it is to do the science better, or to acknowledge that the dogmas of faith have not been "understood and explained in accordance with the mind of the Church."

A good example of this dance between faith and reason can be found in the then-authoritative *Catholic Encyclopedia* on the question of evolution. The *Catholic Encyclopedia*, published in the first decade of the twentieth century, just fifty years after Darwin's *Origin of Species* and twenty years after Vatican I, could find no objection to the theory of evolution on the basis of faith: "It is in perfect agreement with the Christian conception of the universe; for Scripture does not tell us in what form the present species of plants and of animals were originally created by God."[23] It did, however, express caution on the question of the evolution of human beings, leaving to God the question of the source of our "spiritual" aspects, which could not be reduced to mere biological origins. It is also worth recalling that the Augustinian monk Gregor Mendel, with his work in genetic characteristics, provided the mechanism for inheritance that was missing in Darwin's account of evolution and

23. Erich Wasmann, "Catholics and Evolution," in *The Catholic Encyclopedia*, vol. 5 (New York: Robert Appleton Company, 1909). Available at http://www.newadvent.org/cathen/05654a.htm.

formed the basis of the so-called neo-Darwinian synthesis, while the Jesuit scientist Teilhard de Chardin helped discover vital fossil evidence in the evolution of human beings. The positive reception of the notion of biological evolution within Catholic thought has continued in the more recent statement of Pope John Paul II that "new knowledge leads to the recognition of the theory of evolution as more than a hypothesis. It is indeed remarkable that this theory has been progressively accepted by researchers following a series of discoveries in various fields of knowledge."[24]

Barth and Brunner on Natural Theology

The question of the status of natural theology took another turn in the middle of the twentieth century with the debate between two Protestant theologians, Karl Barth and Emil Brunner.[25] Brunner had written on the possibility of a return to natural theology, not as a rationalist stand-alone approach to God, but through a reading of the Christian doctrine of creation. Despite the fallenness of human beings, he argued that some continued analogy existed between the creature and the Creator that could allow for arguments about God's existence and nature. Still, this was a mediating position between an outright rejection of natural theology and those who sought to develop a natural theology apart from Christian revelation. Famously, Barth's response was a strident "No" to the possibility of a natural theology, and a rejection of any analogy of being (or *analogia entis*) between creature and Creator:

24. Pope John Paul II, "Message to the Pontifical Academy of Sciences on Evolution," 1996, available at http://www.ewtn.com/library/PAPALDOC/JP961022.HTM.
25. For an account of the debate, see Alister E. McGrath, *The Open Secret: A New Vision for Natural Theology* (Malden, MA: Blackwell, 2008), 158–64. Barth's prior fierce debate with Catholic theologian Erich Przywara is important background to this later debate. See Keith L. Johnson, *Karl Barth and the Analogia Entis* (London: T & T Clark, 2010).

> If one occupies oneself with real theology one can pass by so-called natural theology only as one would pass by an abyss into which it is inadvisable to step if one does not want to fall. All one can do is to turn one's back upon it as upon the great temptation and source of error, by having nothing to do with it and by making it clear to oneself and to others from time to time why one acts that way.[26]

For Barth, any god known through reason would be nothing but an idol, not the God of Christian revelation.

As various authors have pointed out, Barth's response to Brunner's suggestion was conditioned by the historical context of the rise of Nazism and its impact within the German churches. Barth's central concern was that if faith appealed to anything other than the revelation of God through the Scriptures—for example, either the natural order or the events of human history—then a door would open that would legitimize Nazi claims to represent a new stage in Christian history.[27]

Given Barth's eminence, especially among theologians of the Reformed tradition, his strictures against natural theology continue to resonate among Protestant theologians. In a recent contribution to the debate surrounding natural theology, Andrew Moore concludes that contemporary efforts to develop a natural theology in light of recent debates with secularism and the new atheism are a flawed strategy. There is no halfway house or common ground between Christian faith and the basic stance of these opponents, and to seek to find such common ground is to concede too much:

> It would be ironic if contemporary Christians were to add a further twist to the dialectical relationship between theism and atheism by using natural theology to achieve that reflective rationality which, it is

---

26. Emil Brunner and Karl Barth, *Natural Theology* (London: Geoffrey Bles, 1946), 75, quoted in Andrew Moore, "Should Christians Do Natural Theology?" *Scottish Journal of Theology* 63 (2010): 127–45, at 134, n. 24.

27. See Mark R. Lindsay, *Barth, Israel, and Jesus: Karl Barth's Theology of Israel*, Barth Studies (Hampshire: Ashgate, 2007), for details, esp. chapter 3.

mistakenly supposed, their needing to legitimize their beliefs requires. We might live in a culture that ridicules, or is indifferent to, Christians' epistemic claims, but perhaps the best way to win acceptance for them is not to internalize the contradiction between the two and adopt a defensive stance. Perhaps rather it is to have the confidence imparted by properly theological convictions and accept that there is a humanly unbridgeable gulf between belief and unbelief.[28]

Given a "humanly unbridgeable gulf," no dialogue is possible and one should leave the atheists and secularists to their own devices. The power of the gospel is enough.

Contemporary Approaches

Paradoxically, while natural theology has some traction among contemporary Protestant theologians, it is almost dead in the water for most Catholic theologians. Apart from Hans Küng's comprehensive *Does God Exist?* (written over three decades ago) it is hard to think of a major work by a leading Catholic theologian on the topic.[29] Largely this neglect is a reaction against the type of neo-Scholastic apologetics that dominated Catholic approaches to natural theology prior to the Second Vatican Council. However, there are some approaches that do exist and are worth noting.

Analytic Philosophy

The second half of the twentieth century witnessed a revival of interest in questions of natural theology among analytic philosophers. At the forefront of this revival was Richard Swinburne, who sought

---

28. Moore, "Should Christians Do Natural Theology?" 145.
29. Hans Küng, *Does God Exist? An Answer for Today* (Garden City, NY: Doubleday, 1980). Indeed, the main thrust of Küng's book is to argue that God's existence cannot be proved using reason alone.

to introduce a different form of argument into the debates, one based on Bayesian probability-type arguments.[30] He rejects the possibility of proving deductively that God exists from the fact of the existence of the cosmos, contending that while it may increase the probability of the conclusion, it does not make it more probable than it not being the case that God exists. Rather, he develops a more inductive argument based on notions of simplicity and complexity. This leads him to conclude that the existence of God is the most likely outcome for explaining the existence of our complex universe compared to the denial of God's existence:

> I suggest that theism is very, very much more probable than any other rival personal explanation for the existence, orderliness, and other characteristics of the universe. ... The only plausible alternative to theism is the supposition that the world with all the characteristics which I have described just is, with no explanation. That however is not a very probable alternative.[31]

While many steps removed from the certainty of the metaphysical arguments of Aquinas, Swinburne's high profile gave legitimacy to the quest to develop new approaches to the God question among philosophers.

One should also note Alvin Plantinga's efforts to resurrect Anselm's ontological argument through the use of modal logic and his continued efforts to defend Christian theism.[32] The ontological argument sought to prove the existence of God by defining God as "something than which nothing greater can be thought." It argued

---

30. There are two main schools of thought within statistics. Bayesians seek to assign a probability to the truth or falsity of statements, while frequentists assign a frequency on the basis of empirical data. Under some circumstances they will lead to different conclusions.
31. Richard Swinburne, *The Existence of God* (Oxford/New York: Oxford University Press, 1979), 287.
32. Modal logic seeks to operate not on propositions that express something as just true or false, but as possibly and necessarily true or false. On the ontological argument, see Alvin Plantinga and James F. Sennett, *The Analytic Theist: An Alvin Plantinga Reader* (Grand Rapids: Eerdmans, 1998), 65–71.

that such a being must exist, because if it did not, adding existence would make it greater. Critics, such as Aquinas, argued that there was an illegitimate jump from the intentional order, or order of thought, to the real order of existence in this argument.[33] What Anselm proved was that if God exists, then God exists necessarily, but it does not in fact establish God's existence. Plantinga seeks to overcome this difficulty through a modal logic that bridges the gap between possible existence and necessary existence. This step involves "all possible worlds" arguments common in analytic philosophy, as he contends that if something is possibly true, then its possibility is necessary (it is possibly true in all worlds). However, it is doubtful this argument will convince many. As with Anselm's original argument, it seems to get "something [real] from nothing [but thought]."

Both Swinburne and Plantinga are Christian believers and professionally respected philosophers whose efforts have validated a revival of interest in natural theology. It is of interest to note that the efforts of Swinburne and others have been enough to convince a leading former atheist, Antony Flew, to renounce his atheism and conclude that God does in fact exist.[34]

Perhaps a high point in these efforts is the *Blackwell Companion to Natural Theology*, edited by William Lane Craig and J. P. Moreland.[35] This volume contains detailed discussions that grapple with the findings of contemporary science and philosophical literature to present the best possible arguments for the existence of God. Particularly impressive is the willingness of the authors to engage

---

33. Ironically, Aquinas would agree with Dawkins, who expresses "deep suspicion of any line of reasoning that reached such a significant conclusion without feeding in a single piece of data from the real world" (Dawkins, *The God Delusion*, 82).
34. Antony Flew and Roy Abraham Varghese, *There Is a God: How the World's Most Notorious Atheist Changed His Mind*, 1st ed. (New York: HarperOne, 2007). In the introduction, Flew specifically mentions Swinburne and Brian Leftow as being most helpful in the move (ibid., 3).
35. *The Blackwell Companion to Natural Theology*, ed. William Lane Craig and J. P. Moreland (Oxford: Blackwell, 2009).

with quite serious scientific and mathematical arguments in contemporary cosmology to demonstrate the openness of these scientific findings to a theistic view of the universe. Nonetheless, despite these heroic efforts, one is still left with the sense that, as Taylor has noted, "the inference to the transcendent is at the extreme and most fragile end of a chain of inferences; it is the most epistemically questionable."[36] Certainly these are not "man in the street" arguments, though the broad outlines of the positions are relatively comprehensible to the nonspecialist reader.

Alister McGrath and a "Christian Natural Theology"

In his book *The Open Secret*, Alister McGrath has presented what he calls a "Christian" natural theology.[37] While recognizing hesitations especially among Protestant theologians to the concept of natural theology, McGrath opts for an approach not dissimilar to that of Brunner, seeking to develop a natural theology on the basis of a Christian theology of creation and other doctrines: "A Christian understanding of nature is the intellectual prerequisite for a natural theology which discloses the Christian God."[38] Indeed, this approach does not step away from specifically Christian doctrines; it actually builds upon them. It involves an "engagement with nature that is conducted in the light of a Christian vision of reality, resting on a trinitarian, incarnational ontology."[39] More forcefully, McGrath's vision of natural theology "derives its legitimization and mandate from within the Christian tradition, rather than from some allegedly 'universal' general principles."[40] What this means in practice is the

---

36. Taylor, *A Secular Age*, 558.
37. McGrath, *The Open Secret*.
38. Ibid., 4.
39. Ibid., 6.
40. Ibid., 171.

liberal use of biblical texts, notably from Old Testament Wisdom literature, to argue for the legitimacy of a natural theological approach that discloses the Christian God. The controlling motif, however, remains its Christian orientation: "If the God who is disclosed through the natural world is not the same as the God who is revealed in Christ, then it has little relevance to the tasks of Christian theology."[41]

While McGrath provides an interesting example of the way Christians might think about the issue of natural theology in dialogue with other Christians (an intra-ecclesial context), it is not clear that his approach would appeal to non-Christian theists (for example, Jewish or Muslim believers in an interreligious context) or allow for entry into a public arena of debate with atheists or secularists. By setting a high bar for entry (explicitly Christian doctrines), he excludes believers from non-Christian religious traditions (and of course nonbelievers) from the conversation, and would find himself excluded from a broader audience. Nonetheless, in other works McGrath has added considerably to the debate, taking on various champions of the new atheism in an effective manner.[42]

Bernard Lonergan and the Intelligibility of Reality

While not often noticed outside a circle of specialist scholars, Bernard Lonergan has made significant contributions to the natural theology debate. In fact, in *New Proofs for the Existence of God*, Robert Spitzer devoted an entire chapter to Lonergan's proof of the existence of

---

41. Ibid., 213.
42. See, for example, the following works: Alister E. McGrath, *Dawkins' God: Genes, Memes, and the Meaning of Life* (Malden, MA: Blackwell, 2005); Alister E. McGrath and Joanna McGrath, *The Dawkins Delusion: Atheist Fundamentalism and the Denial of the Divine* (Downers Grove, IL: InterVarsity Press, 2007); McGrath, *A Fine-Tuned Universe: The Quest for God in Science and Theology*, 1st ed. (Louisville: Westminster John Knox, 2009).

God, albeit in a transposed mode.[43] In chapter 19 of his major philosophical work, *Insight*, Lonergan develops the basic components of his natural theology, including a proof of the existence of God.[44] This proof comes at the end of a process that Lonergan describes as a "moving viewpoint." Lonergan begins with the cognitional question ("What am I doing when I know?"), then moves onto the epistemological question ("Why is doing that knowing?"), to conclude with the metaphysical question ("What do I know when I know?").

In addressing the cognitional question, Lonergan draws from examples in mathematics and science, not in terms of their outcomes, but in terms of the process of reasoning they use to arrive at their outcomes. Central to his account is the act of insight, where we move from not understanding a particular phenomenon, through the tension of questioning and inquiry, to the release of that tension in an inner act of understanding. Lonergan claims that this act of insight is the foundation of all mathematical and scientific advances. By distinguishing different types of insight, Lonergan is able to ground both classical scientific theories such as theories of classical mechanics and gravitation (Newton, Einstein) and statistical scientific theories such as quantum mechanics and evolution. Indeed, Lonergan combines these two types of theories to develop an account of what he calls "schemes of recurrence," cyclic patterns of events that form the basis for an emergent probability of higher and higher schemes.

43. Robert J. Spitzer, *New Proofs for the Existence of God: Contributions of Contemporary Physics and Philosophy* (Grand Rapids: Eerdmans, 2010). Spitzer transposes Lonergan's cognitional and epistemological starting points to an ontological starting point. I would also note the work of Bernard Tyrrell, *Bernard Lonergan's Philosophy of God* (Notre Dame, IN: University of Notre Dame Press, 1974).
44. Bernard J. F. Lonergan, *Insight: A Study of Human Understanding*, ed. Crowe Frederick E. and Robert M. Doran, Collected Works of Bernard Lonergan 3 (Toronto: University of Toronto Press, 1992).

This account provides a general framework for phenomena such as evolution.[45]

Significantly, Lonergan's approach allows for a proper distinction between science and metaphysics. While science is concerned with understanding empirical data, metaphysics is concerned with the structure of the known in general, as revealed by the structure of knowing. This allows us to think of metaphysics as properly a meta-discipline that is concerned with the structure of scientific knowledge, rather than the content of that knowing. It is an examination of the structure of knowing and the known, rather than the content, that then raises questions about the whole of reality. For example, science presupposes that reality is susceptible to human understanding. This presupposition is verified with every scientific success. Yet it remains a presupposition that science itself never addresses. As Einstein once commented, "The most incomprehensible thing about the universe is that it is comprehensible."[46] Such an observation marks a shift to a metaphysical stance.

This shift to a metaphysical stance is the entry point to Lonergan's approach to natural theology. Lonergan summarizes his proof for the existence of God with the following syllogism:

If the real is completely intelligible, God exists.

But the real is completely intelligible.

Therefore God exists.[47]

While this may not make sense to the reader at this stage, the next two chapters of this book will work to make it more comprehensible.

---

45. See Neil Ormerod and Cynthia S. W. Crysdale, *Creator God, Evolving World* (Minneapolis: Fortress Press, 2013), for details.
46. Albert Einstein, *Ideas and Opinions*, trans. Sonja Bargmann (New York: Bonanza, 1954), 292.
47. Lonergan, *Insight*, 695.

Here it will be enough to note that the issue of the intelligibility of reality is not a scientific question, though it is presupposed by the scientific method, but properly one that arises from a metaphysical stance.

Lonergan's proof, then, is the cumulative outcome of a moving viewpoint that begins with the cognitional self-appropriation of the knower, using examples drawn from mathematics and science, and moves through the epistemological and metaphysical consequences of that appropriation. Inasmuch as one is taken along that path, the conclusion may be rationally compelling, but the journey is as important as the destination. As Lonergan notes of his own struggle to reach up to the mind of Aquinas, "The reaching had changed me profoundly [and] . . . the change was the essential benefit."[48]

While still a conclusion "at the extreme and most fragile end of a chain of inferences,"[49] Lonergan's argument does add something that is often missed in the debate over natural theology. People come to any argument for the existence of God with certain presuppositions about the meaning of key terms such as *existence* and *real*. If, for example, one means by *existence*, "existence in space and time," or by *real*, "material things," then arguments for the existence of God that lead to a nonspatiotemporal, nonmaterial being will never have traction. As Lonergan notes, "One cannot prove the existence of God to a Kantian without first breaking his allegiance to Kant. One cannot prove the existence of God to a positivist without first converting him from positivism."[50] Such a process can never be the result of logic alone, which presumes some univocal control of meaning. What is required is a shift from one construction of

48. Ibid., 769.
49. Taylor, *A Secular Age*, 558.
50. Bernard J. F. Lonergan, "The General Character of the Natural Theology of Insight," in *Philosophical and Theological Papers 1965–1980*, ed. R. M. Doran and Frederick E. Crowe, Collected Works of Bernard Lonergan 17 (Toronto: University of Toronto Press, 2004), 6.

meaning of such key terms as *existence* and *real* to another construction of meaning. This shift is so radical that Lonergan refers to it as "intellectual conversion." While the language of conversion may sound religious, for Lonergan the process remains basically a philosophical shift. We shall consider this in more detail in the next two chapters.

Conclusion

What does this survey of the literature on natural theology tell us about the present project? It tells us, first, that any attempt at a natural theology is likely to be attacked from both sides: from atheists and secularists who argue that science has eliminated the need for God and that public appeals to God should be relegated to the realm of the irrational and fanciful;[51] and from fellow believers who insist that reason alone can only lead us astray to belief in false gods, not the God of revelation.

Yet there is a long intellectual tradition—one that predates Christianity, but that Christianity took into its heart—that sees some value in the project. The God question continues to be raised. It is here that I would differentiate the present project from the work of McGrath. He describes his work as a "Christian natural theology," whereas I would describe this work as one of "natural theology in the Christian tradition." It may draw on themes and insights from the Christian tradition of attempts at natural theology, but it will not draw on Christian sources as authoritative or normative. In that way, I hope to capture the insight in Lonergan's seemingly paradoxical statement, "I do not think that in this life people arrive at natural knowledge of God without God's grace, but what I do not doubt is that the knowledge they so attain is natural."[52]

---

51. One regularly finds derogatory comments comparing belief in God with "an invisible friend," "a fairy at the bottom of the garden," or a "flying spaghetti monster."

However, it is also worth stating what this work does not try to achieve. It is not trying to argue people into Christian faith, though at times my Christian orientation will be more evident. Many religions believe in the existence of one God, and a work in natural theology does not provide a means of adjudicating competing religious claims. On the other hand, if natural theology can work to open up a public space for the discussion and respect for religion, it does so in a way that leaves such theistic religions on a level playing field. Such a public space cannot then become a battleground for competing religious claims based on special revelation.

Nor is natural theology likely on its own to convert atheists and secularists from pursuing their agendas. As John Henry Newman once commented, "first shoot round corners, and you may not despair of converting by a syllogism."[53] Conversion is never just an intellectual process; personal contact and relationships are far more important than what will be found in the present work. On the other hand, it seems to me that there is some point in arguing that belief in God's existence is publicly and rationally defensible, if only so believers may not lose heart under the relentless barrage of antireligious sentiments that seem to dominate our media and culture.

52. Lonergan, "Natural Knowledge of God," 133.
53. John Henry Newman, *An Essay in Aid of a Grammar of Assent* (London: Burns, Oates and Co., 1874), 73.

2

———

God, Proof, and Reason

In the first chapter, we explored the question of how we might think of the natural theology project. Central to that project is the task of seeking to prove the existence of God. Yet one of the often-unexplored questions around this task is the very notion of proof itself. What does it mean to "prove" something? Proof often depends on a number of factors—the shared background meanings of those listening, the presentation of evidence, the use of reasoning, and so on—that move us from uncertainty to a conclusion to which we feel rationally compelled to assent. Further, we recognize that different contexts may require a different degree of rigor in proof: for the juror in court it must be "beyond a reasonable doubt"; the mathematician requires absolute deductive rigor; for the scientist it is usually a question of the best available evidence matching a given hypothesis. And, of course, proof depends on the meanings we give to the terms of our argument. This is why mathematics is so successful in expanding its findings. Mathematics, and to a lesser degree, science, is able to tightly control the meaning of its key terms and relations. Once such a tight control of meaning is not present, absolute deductive rigor is no longer possible.

All this is important to keep in mind when approaching the question of proving the existence of God. We might have a commonsense apprehension of what is meant by the term *God* (a fatherly figure in "heaven"), or we might have a more philosophically refined meaning of the term (subsistent being) that sits at some variance with a commonsense apprehension. Which "existence" are we seeking to prove? Further, an opponent might claim that the notion of God is incoherent or self-contradictory, and so no being with the standard list of divine attributes could possibly exist. Often the existence of evil will be invoked to suggest that God's existence, with certain specified attributes, is incompatible with evil. But questions always remain about what those attributes might mean when applied to God.

In the end, then, context matters in seeking to do natural theology. In a context that more or less takes the existence of God for granted, the task of proving the existence of God will not be so demanding as it would be in a context where there is widespread skepticism, such as we find today. Of course, there is always the danger of thinking that one's own context is the norm, but the present day has its own set of historical circumstances, the cumulative product of its past, scientifically and philosophically.

These are some of the issues we need to explore in the present chapter. After a brief excursus on culture, we will begin with an account of the shifting cultural context surrounding Aquinas's attempts to prove the existence of God. This acts as a reminder that his context is not ours. We will then turn to our own context to explore at greater depth the two fairly dominant paradigms of mathematics and the empirical sciences. While similar, these are not the same, and the differences encourage us to consider the possibility of a different paradigm—what I shall call a metaphysical paradigm—as a cultural condition for the possibility of a genuine natural theology.

Why should such a paradigm be needed? Because the unspoken issue of the nature of proof is why proof actually proves anything at all. Proving something is a complex intellectual process: having insights, forming hypotheses, gathering evidence, and coming to a conclusion. Why do we assume that this process tell us something about reality? Implicit in the process of proving is the notion that reality is susceptible to reason, or in Lonergan's shorthand, "The real is completely intelligible."[1] Grasping the connection between truth in the mind (as the outcome of a process of reasoning) and reality (as independent of the mind) is the starting point of intellectual conversion. While these are questions we have lost sight of in our present culture, such issues were well known within the cultural horizon of Aquinas.

An Excursus on Culture

In order to pursue the argument I wish to develop in this chapter, I will need to introduce a helpful distinction from the writings of Robert Doran,[2] who himself is drawing on the work of the political philosopher Eric Voegelin.[3] Doran introduces a dialectical structure into the notion of culture—that is, a structure with two linked but opposed principles that drive a process of change. Culture, understood empirically, is a set of meanings and values by which a community makes sense of and orders its world. Doran identifies

---

1. Bernard J. F. Lonergan, *Insight: A Study of Human Understanding*, ed. Frederick E. Crowe and Robert M. Doran, Collected Works of Bernard Lonergan 3 (Toronto: University of Toronto Press, 1992), 659.

2. Robert M. Doran, *Theology and the Dialectics of History* (Toronto: University of Toronto Press, 1990).

3. Eric Voegelin, *The New Science of Politics: An Introduction* (Chicago: University of Chicago Press, 1952).

two cultural types, which he calls cosmological and anthropological cultures. These are ideal types, two distinct poles of a dialectic, with actual cultures exhibiting elements of each to various degrees of sophistication and depth.

The cosmological pole of the cultural dialectic is marked by attunement to the rhythms and cycles of nature, by a sense of cosmic participation through which the individual is ordered to the society and the society to the cosmic hierarchy. Human destiny is viewed as subject to cosmic forces beyond our control, and human flourishing requires our conformity to the cosmic order. Hunter-gatherer people such as Australian Aboriginal peoples and the First Nation peoples of North America display these features, as do more settled rural and agricultural societies. This pole of the cultural dialectic remains a permanently valid source of meaning and value for any society. Taken on its own, however, it tends to fatalism, pantheism, the stifling of the individual, and a static conception of social order that is trapped within a static cosmic order.

The anthropological pole of the cultural dialectic seeks to order the society to the individual and the individual to a world-transcendent source of meaning and value. Rather than the individual conforming to society, society is measured by its responsiveness to the individual. Individual initiative is encouraged and promoted. Human existence and society is ordered not by cosmic forces but by reason. For example, we can see some of the transition from the cosmological to the anthropological pole in the shift from monarchies—as bearers of a divine right to rule based on the arbitrary privilege of birth—to democratic and republican structures where majority rules and meritocracy prevails. The breakthrough into anthropological meaning is also evident in the emergence of philosophy in the ancient Greeks, of Scholasticism in the Middle Ages, science in the modern era, and so on. Cut off from cosmological sources of meaning and value, anthropological culture tends to undervalue the natural order, leading to the destruction of the environment and the denigration of "primitive" cultures.

I shall make use of these notions of cosmological and anthropological culture in analyzing some of the context within which natural theology is located. I believe they help us understand something of the shift that occurred during the Middle Ages and is happening in our present context of modernity and postmodernity, as well as helping us understand the correctives that need to be put in place to overcome present cultural distortions. One such corrective is, I believe, the return of natural theology to more active consideration within theological circles.

Thomas Aquinas and the "Five Ways"

The Middle Ages were a high point for natural theology. The "five ways" of Thomas Aquinas (*Summa Theologiae* [henceforth *ST*] I 2.3) have made an indelible impression upon all subsequent attempts to prove the existence of God. However we understand the impact of this effort in subsequent history, it is also necessary to place it within its own time and culture.

The High Middle Ages was a time of profound social and cultural shifts. Moving out of an era of social and economic stagnation, Europe was becoming increasingly urbanized, with a developing middle class of merchants and traders. As cities grew, new institutions emerged such as the university, a sure sign of surplus wealth and growing cultural reflection. New learning that centered on the naturalistic philosophy of Aristotle began to dominate theological speculation, displacing the more neoplatonic approach of the church fathers. The tensions between these two approaches are well known and produced significant debate at the time.

However, I would like to suggest another aspect to these shifts, evident in the distinction I referred to above between cosmological and anthropological cultures. The movement from rural to urban settings, from agricultural to manufactured goods, from subsistence to a trading economy, also initiates a movement from a more cosmologically oriented culture to one that is more anthropologically oriented. A rural, agricultural, and subsistence society is more attuned to the rhythms of nature, its cycles and moods. Its closeness to the natural environment is more likely to find the divine within the natural order, and so promote a sense of participation in divine presence through the natural world. Within such a worldview, the existence of God is hardly an issue; indeed, it is almost taken as self-evident. The whole of creation reflects the glory of God, and God's existence is apparent in that glory. Of course, the downside of this type of participatory experience is the identification of God with the natural order, a pantheism that the Catholic Church at the time associated with paganism.

However, the movement to an urban, manufacturing, trading society means a movement into a world that is much more the product of human practicality and intelligence. Human beings become less subject to the rhythms and cycles of nature and more subject to the demands of practicality, to time as measured by clocks and calendars, to a spatiality dominated by human constructions rather than the natural environment. There is a confidence in human intelligence to at least mollify, if not control, the natural order, and certainly in the human ability to understand nature, as expressed in the newly rediscovered philosophy and natural science of Aristotle.

This movement from a more cosmologically to a more anthropologically oriented culture raises fundamental questions about what is the ultimate "measure" of all things. In a cosmological culture, the individual is ordered to the society and the society to the cosmic order, the divine court. God is thus the ultimate measure, though in its "pagan" distortion this measure may be equated with nature itself. In an anthropological culture, society is ordered to the individual and the individual to some world-transcending measure, such as God or reason. The question then is, What is the basis for this world-transcending measure? Is it human reason itself by which all things are to be measured? Or is the ultimate world-transcending measure to be found in the ground of all reason, an ungrounded reason of which human reason is a pale and limited participation?

Placed in this context, the "five ways" of Aquinas take on a different significance. Taken ahistorically, they have been read as a preamble to faith, a high point of Christian apologetic. However, taken contextually they are an attempt to face a major cultural issue of the day: as we move to a more anthropological culture, do we necessarily abandon our sense of God? Can we discard God as an unnecessary hypothesis to be replaced by human reason, or does human reason itself lead us with some inevitability to God? Aquinas's response is that human reason does in fact lead us to God, that human reason is itself to be measured against divine reason, which is the ultimate source of reason and order in the cosmos.

We might begin with a consideration of *ST* I 2.1, where Aquinas asks "whether the existence of God is self-evident?" In the first objection, he notes the position of John Damascene that "the knowledge of God is naturally implanted in all." He does not dismiss the existence of such knowledge but speaks of it as general and confused, "implanted in us by nature, inasmuch as God is man's beatitude." However, "this . . . is not to know absolutely that God exists," since it is not the outcome of a reasoned argument, which is properly constitutive of knowing. Rather, it is a form of participatory knowledge, which is commonly experienced in a more cosmological culture. Aquinas then goes on to ask in *ST* I 2.2 whether the existence of God is "demonstrable," that is, can be obtained as the conclusion of a reasonable argument. In this, he clears the ground by eliminating arguments that reject the possibility of demonstrating the existence of God, in particular the argument that God's existence can be known only by faith. Finally, in *ST* I 2.3 he sets out his "five ways" for demonstrating the existence of God: from motion, from efficient causality, from contingency and necessity, from the graded hierarchy of beings, and from the governance of the world. In each of these he identifies some aspect of the created order that remains unexplained without reference to some higher-order, creation-transcending cause. In all this, we find a simultaneous confidence in reason—in its ability to establish the existence of God—and a subordination of human reason to that of God. Further, the participatory sense of mystery found in a more cosmological culture and acknowledged in *ST* I 2.1 is shown not to be pure illusion, but something that reason itself may graciously acknowledge: "And this all people call God."

Aquinas's proofs are little more than sketches of arguments whose presuppositions and background resources would have been known to and possessed by his intended audience. As *ST* was written as a "beginner's" textbook in theology, Aquinas could presume that his readers were grounded in the basics of metaphysics and could easily fill in the blanks for themselves. This is no longer the case, as Dawkins's two-page dismissal of Aquinas reveals. Dawkins concludes, "The five 'proofs' asserted by Thomas Aquinas in the thirteenth century don't prove anything, and are easily—though I hesitate to say so given his eminence—exposed as vacuous."[4] What in fact is exposed is Dawkins's complete lack of the orientations and skills needed to make sense of what Aquinas is arguing.

4. Richard Dawkins, *The God Delusion* (London: Bantam, 2006), 77.

A good example of how such shifting contexts change the meaning of terms can be found by considering Aquinas's proof from "motion." We read the term "motion" and think in terms of physical movement, of particles in space and time moving about, perhaps of Newton's laws or something more sophisticated. Aquinas thinks in terms of change from potency to act, as illustrated, for example, when we come to understand something in an insight. This is not motion as we moderns understand it, but it is a change; and it is closer to what Aquinas meant by the term "motion" than physical movement.

Our Current Context

Where does this leave us now? While Aquinas was dealing with a shift from a cosmologically oriented culture to one with a greater contribution from anthropological meanings and value, anthropological culture now dominates our horizon. Indeed, we could argue that we live in a society that is feeling the effects of a long-term cultural imbalance in the direction of anthropological culture, given by many commentators the name of "modernity." It has actively promoted the faith-reason split, the exploitation of the natural environment for commercial ends, the destruction of indigenous peoples and cultures, the subservience of science (as a mode of domination and control of the natural world) to the economy, and an overarching belief in progress driven by technological solutions to human problems. While there is widespread disenchantment with this cultural form, it remains dominant in our social and cultural life.[5]

---

5. Culture is of course a complex notion. For a solid exposition see Kathryn Tanner, *Theories of Culture: A New Agenda for Theology* (Minneapolis: Fortress Press, 1997). Culture rarely if ever speaks with a single voice; there are competing and at times subversive voices alongside the dominant form. For example, over the centuries there have been outbursts of romantic idealism to compensate for the one-sidedness of our anthropological orientation. Nonetheless, I would

The disenchantment takes two major forms. The first is postmodernism. Postmodernism involves rejecting the "master narrative" of modernity, raising the counter-voices of minority and repressed traditions, and calling into question the value of reason as a world-transcendent source of meaning. All claims to reason and argument are taken as attempts to exert power over the other. They are evidence of a "will to power" and must be deconstructed, usually by a genealogical critique that reduces all argument to special pleading or personal interest. Postmodernism leads to disenchantment with reason itself, a position that I think is in the end a counsel of despair.

The movement from modernity to postmodernity has parallels in the medieval movement from the conceptualism of Scotus to the nominalism of Ockham. Conceptualism thought that the concepts of the mind were universal and necessary. The discovery of the contingency of those concepts led to the skepticism of Ockham, the rejection of metaphysics, and the assertion of particularity. In our own era, postmodernism has likewise discovered the contingency of reason and has responded by rejecting its totalizing claims and promoting particularity. Now it is not metaphysics that is suspect, having long been rejected by modernity itself, but science and technology.

Indeed, there may be some common ground between believers and atheists in relation to postmodernism. In the end, the relativism of postmodernism is no friend of either religious belief (though postmodernism may tolerate it) or the claims of scientific reason. Though atheists may lump believers with postmoderns as both "off with the fairies" in relation to reason, the position developed in this

---

argue that over the past half a millennium the anthropological culture has dominated to the increasing exclusion of the cosmological.

present work would likewise express concern at the undermining of reason present in postmodernism.

The other form that disenchantment with modernity has taken is the reemergence of cosmological sources of meaning and value. This is found in a renewed appreciation of indigenous cultures, which are much more oriented to the cosmological pole of the cultural dialectic, and in the growing environmental movement, which seeks to protect the natural world and prevent ecological destruction.[6] Some of this is expressed in a type of re-enchantment of the natural world, a renewed sense of the sacred in nature and of divine immanence to creation that is characteristic of earlier romantic rejections of the rationalism of modernity.

However, Doran's analysis of the cultural dialectic would suggest that this movement is of itself not enough. Cut off from cosmological meanings, anthropological culture is distorted. In modernity, this is evident in the instrumentalization of reason, its subordination to practicality, and the ruling out of metaphysics. In this context, it is not enough to reaffirm cosmological meanings and value; it is also important to provide an intellectual therapeutic for reason itself. Reason needs to recover its primordial orientation to truth and reality as an act of resistance to its subordination to practicality (modernity) on the one hand, or its subversion to the will to power (postmodernity) on the other.

It is in this environment that I would like to specify something of the current context and purpose of natural theology. Our situation has similarities and differences to that of Aquinas. In the face of a transition from a more cosmological to a more anthropological culture, Aquinas's "five ways" were a statement of both confidence

---

6. This is particularly evident in the writings and other media productions of David Suzuki. In particular, see David Suzuki and Peter Knudson, *Wisdom of the Elders: Honoring Sacred Native Visions of Nature* (New York: Bantam, 1992).

in human reason and its subordination to divine reason. It affirmed the religious meanings of a cosmological culture, but helped ensure that the notion of God was not to be reduced to nature. Our context is more complex. Our hyper-anthropological culture has lost touch with cosmological meanings. Its persistent instrumentalizing of reason has led to a loss of confidence in, or at the very least a truncation of, reason itself. Indeed, the more successful reason has become in analyzing the material world, the more we have restricted its validity to that field alone. Our culture needs not just a restoration of cosmological meanings but a renewal of reason. A contextual natural theology rejects the instrumentalizing of reason, its subordination to practicality. It affirms the primordial orientation of reason to truth and reality; but far from being an act of hubris or will to power, its goal is the location of human reason within a larger framework of divine reason, of which it is a limited finite participation. So conceived, a natural theology will also ensure that the reaffirmation of cosmological meaning and value will not result in a reduction of God to the natural world.

All this is by way of reminding ourselves of the importance of context. Our conceptions of reason are historically conditioned.[7] Different eras and contexts have different expectations about what constitutes a reasoned argument. In a cosmologically oriented culture, appeals to traditional authorities constitute an accepted form of reasoning. The greater the impact of anthropologically oriented meanings and values, the greater the focus on the individual's capacity to reason for herself, and so Kant extolled his readers to "dare to think."

Still, the form of what is accepted as "reasonable" depends on certain paradigmatic conceptions of reason operative at the time,

---

7. This important point is well made by Alasdair MacIntyre in *Whose Justice? Which Rationality?* (Notre Dame, IN: University of Notre Dame Press, 1988).

and such conceptions of reason are often at variance with the actual performance of the reasoning subject. We now consider two such paradigmatic expressions of reason—one mathematical, the other scientific—to see what light, if any, they may shed on the question of what it might mean to prove the existence of God.

A Mathematical Paradigm

Mathematics provides us with a powerful and compelling cultural paradigm for the notion of proof. I can still remember as a young teenager being presented with a proof of the irrationality of the square root of two. Here was an argument, which a teenager could follow, that definitively established the truth of a certain proposition. A similar experience can be found in an initial exposure to Euclidean geometry.[8] There is something overwhelming in recognizing the power of reasoned argument to prove that something is or is not the case. Yet even at that age it was evident to me that the power of the argument was more evident to some than to others. While some found it natural to think along such lines, others clearly found it more difficult.

And the more one progresses in mathematics, the more difficult things become. One of the sources of difficulty is the amount of rigor required at any particular stage of a proof; thus Bertrand Russell and Alfred North Whitehead took several hundred pages of their monumental work *Principia Mathematica* to produce a proof that "1+1=2."[9] Starting from the minimal assumptions of set theory, it took

8. For an account of its impact on Thomas Hobbes see Michael Allen Gillespie, *The Theological Origins of Modernity* (Chicago: University of Chicago Press, 2008), 216.
9. Alfred North Whitehead and Bertrand Russell, *Principia Mathematica* (Cambridge: Cambridge University Press, 1910), 379.

some time before they could define numbers and addition to arrive at this basic conclusion, known to every child.

Of course, in practice mathematicians rarely display such an absolute (or dare one say obsessive) concern for rigor, but nonetheless a proof might be a monumental cultural achievement. Perhaps the best-known recent example is Andrew Wiles's proof of "Fermat's last theorem."[10] The problem, first proposed in 1637 by French mathematician Pierre de Fermat, concerned the existence or nonexistence of integer solutions to a certain class of equations. Some 350 years after it was conjectured, Wiles published a definitive solution to the problem. While one cannot detract from the genius displayed by Wiles, this proof would not have been possible without the ongoing collaboration of hundreds of mathematicians in the intervening centuries who contributed something to the final solution, some positively, others negatively by eliminating false paths. Wiles was not starting from scratch, nor was he required to recreate or reprove all that had been done before. And when his proof was finally published, there may have been a handful of mathematicians in the world who really understood it and could have verified its validity.

This brief excursus illuminates a number of points. While mathematics appeals to the rationality of its operations, this appeal is not without a particular context. Apart from the rationality of the human subject, one also requires a basic disposition or orientation to the subject matter, which disposition becomes more refined and demanding the further along the path one goes. What is obvious to one person may be far from obvious to another. And even with fairly

10. For those interested in an accessible account of the problem and its history I would suggest Simon Singh, *Fermat's Last Theorem: The Story of a Riddle that Confounded the World's Greatest Minds for 358 Years* (London: Fourth Estate, 1998). There is a theological connection here. Andrew Wiles's father was the well-known theologian and patristic scholar Maurice Wiles (1923–2005).

refined mathematical sensibilities, one may be misled. In the history of Fermat's last theorem there is no shortage of failed proofs that stood, however briefly, before the fault was identified. Fermat himself thought he had a proof that undoubtedly was simply wrong.

This illustrates a further aspect, which is the collaborative and self-correcting nature of the cultural enterprise we call mathematics. We do not trust the work of the individual mathematician so much as of the mathematical community as a whole. Wiles's proof was checked and rechecked by the few who could understand it. Nonetheless, once such a process has been sufficiently undertaken it would be churlish to call its validity into question. While some in that community could follow Wiles's proof, the rest believed in the self-correcting process of peer review to operate and weed out error.

A further point is that mathematics is often concerned with questions of existence or nonexistence. Mathematicians will seek to establish the existence or nonexistence of various mathematical objects—numbers, groups, fields, rings, topological spaces and so on—that satisfy various conditions or constraints. Here we can identify a connection between reasoned argument and questions of existence, or between truth and reality. On one side we have the reasoning processes of the human subject, on the other some claim to existence. Of course, there can be philosophical debate on the ontological status of such mathematical objects (Do mathematicians discover or invent?), but whatever the outcome of this debate some relationship is being drawn between the reasoning of the subject and the existence of an object.[11] However, proving the existence

---

11. Philosophically, mathematicians may be Platonists, or constructivists, or realists of various types. However, in practice it seems to make little difference to the end result. See, for example, John Burgess and Gideon Rosen, *A Subject with No Object* (Oxford: Oxford University Press, 1997), for current debates, though their contribution is mitigated by their nominalist approach. For Lonergan's account of mathematical judgments and of the objects these intend, see Lonergan, *Insight*, 334–39.

of, for example, a "locally compact abelian group" with a specified "topology"[12] seems somewhat removed from the question of the existence of God.

What do we learn from this mathematical excursus about the problem of proving the existence of God? Two points are important. The first is that while something may be rationally compelling, that does not mean it is obvious or that everyone will get the point. A mathematical proof may be hellishly complex, something accessible only to a thoroughly trained mind. It may require a certain refined orientation or disposition for its compelling nature to become apparent. When it comes to the question of the existence of God, might we not expect it also to require certain orientations or dispositions for its compelling nature to be apparent? Certainly, we might need to discard the assumption that any "person on the street" should be able to follow the argument. Something more than common sense may be required.

The second point is the relationship between reason and being. While the ontological status of mathematical objects remains a question for further investigation, nonetheless mathematicians certainly think they are proving, using reason, the existence or nonexistence of something! In recognizing this connection between reason and existence there is the beginning of a metaphysical orientation.

A Scientific Paradigm

While mathematics is for many an esoteric realm, the world of science appears more tangible and concrete. Science deals with things that "really" exist: subatomic particles and atoms, chemicals, planets,

12. The example is one drawn from many provided in a solid undergraduate program in mathematics. Each of the terms here has a very precise, univocal meaning within mathematics.

rocks, plants, and so on. Moreover, science has transformed human living through the technological spin-offs that have emerged from scientific research. For these reasons, science has a very high level of cultural authority as a paradigm of reason. Scientists play on this authority when they use it to speak outside their field of expertise, taking with them an authority they do not necessarily deserve. Be that as it may, there is considerable public sympathy to the view that science has either rendered religion irrelevant or even "proved" that God is unnecessary for an understanding of the world. The sales of Dawkins's book *The God Delusion* are clear evidence of the popularity of such an opinion.[13]

Of course, reason is very important in science. But the form of reasoning found in science is different from that of mathematics, even while drawing upon mathematics for some of its formulations. While mathematics draws conclusions from premises, science relies on data. However, contra positivist claims, science is not just the accumulation of data but the conjunction of data and theory to lead to a provisional scientific judgment; this conjunction of theoretical hypothesis and empirical verification constitutes scientific reasoning or method. Where a mathematician seeks logical consistency with premises, the scientist seeks verification of hypotheses with empirical data. What gives science its power is the discovery of a theoretical stance that integrates a vast field of data within a single overarching perspective. And so Newton's mathematical account of gravity provided in a few mathematical equations a theoretical framework for rendering intelligible the motion of the planets, and Darwin's theory of evolution provided a theoretical framework for rendering intelligible the diversity-yet-underlying-unity of biological species.

---

13. It also makes frequent appearances on the Internet, where bloggers regularly proclaim the incompatibility of science and religion, often in a most vociferous and at times offensive manner.

Such a theoretical perspective allows science to make predictions that go beyond the present data, to say what will happen or what should or should not exist.[14] Theory provides a hypothetical framework, which must then be verified by the empirical data. If the data does not fit, or if predictions fail to eventuate, then eventually the theory will need revision.[15]

There are a number of things to note about the process outlined above. The first and perhaps most important is the hypothetical nature of scientific work. A scientific theory requires verification in the data. But the data is always approximate, capable of further refinement, and essentially limited. New data may emerge at any time that may or may not conform to the theory. While a given theory may match the available data, one cannot rule out the possibility that new data may emerge that falsifies the existing account or requires its adjustment. For some, this element of falsifiability is the defining characteristic of scientific theory.[16] But this should not be overplayed. Scientists are as interested in verifying as in falsifying a theory. The verification by Arthur Eddington of Einstein's prediction of the bending of light by gravity was a scientific landmark.[17] Similarly, the results from the Large Hadron Collider establishing the existence of the Higgs boson, confirming a

14. One of the more remarkable predictions made by Darwin was the existence of a certain type of moth with a 35cm proboscis, needed to fertilize the orchid known as "Darwin's orchid." Eventually the moth was discovered, after much skepticism as to its existence. See G. Kritsky, "Darwin's Madagascan Hawk Moth Prediction," *American Entomologist* 37 (2001): 206–10.

15. Of course, "fitting" is relative. Newton's account of gravitation remains useful for an account of planetary motion despite its failure to account for the advancing perihelion of Mercury. This phenomenon can be accounted for by Einstein's theory of general relativity. However, for many purposes the mathematically simpler account of Newton is sufficient to give sound results.

16. The role of falsifiability in science was enunciated in Karl R. Popper, *Conjectures and Refutations: The Growth of Scientific Knowledge* (New York: Basic Books, 1962).

17. More recently, the 1993 Nobel Prize in physics was given to Russell A. Hulse and Joseph H. Taylor Jr. for proving the existence of gravitation waves through measurements of decaying orbits of a binary pulsar system, once again providing empirical verification for Einstein's theory of general relativity.

key element of the "Standard Model" in particle physics, caused many champagne bottles to be opened. However, overall it means that scientific judgment always carries the rider: "Best account at present." This distinguishes mathematical judgment from scientific judgment. No one would have cheered had someone argued that Fermat's last theorem was "likely to be true" or that it fitted all available evidence.[18] Proof was required. Science rarely proves its theories definitively; rather, it gives the best account available on a current theory and supporting evidence.

Does this mean science is never definitive? Again, one must not overplay this stance. As the two examples above indicate, there are times when definitive questions of existence/occurrence and nonexistence/nonoccurrence are of profound scientific interest. When Edwin Hubble measured the deflection of light passing by a star, just as Einstein predicted, there was definitive proof of the phenomenon. He proved light bent, as had been predicted. Without the theory, Hubble would have uncovered a puzzling phenomenon, something without explanation. He would have data for something, but proof of nothing. By bringing together the data with Einstein's theory of general relativity, he proved that gravity bends light. Similarly, in proving the existence of the Higgs boson, we have a definite truth that any replacement theory to the Standard Model must take into account. It fills in a missing piece of the Standard Model without which all that would have been found is data waiting to be understood. So science can deal with questions of existence in a definitive matter, through the bringing together of a theoretical framework and empirical data leading to a scientific conclusion.

A second important feature is the culturally collaborative nature of the exercise. Once a theory is proposed, it becomes communal

---

18. In fact, there were proofs available that did something along these lines. While a remarkable achievement, such work never got to the heart of the matter, as in Wiles's eventual proof.

property. It is available for others to explore, examine, verify, and falsify. Newton's success was taken up, applied, and extended by any number of mathematical physicists, and Darwin's theory by any number of biological scientists. And the skills involved often differ. Einstein proposed general relativity, but it was Hubble who verified one of its key predictions. The theoretical physicists who proposed the "Standard Model" are a different breed from those who work the massive particle colliders that test the model's theoretical constructs. These two breeds often require quite different sets of skills to perform their tasks. Again, our confidence in the work of scientists lies in this culture of cross checking, testing, and verification that is essential to scientific progress.[19] Such a process is constitutive of the habitual orientation of the scientist.

A third feature concerns a key difference between mathematics and science. Because science depends on the bringing together of theory and data, there is a constant temptation to make the data fit the theory. Mathematicians may be mistaken in their conclusions, but they are not as open to fraud.[20] Science, however, has had to deal with a steady if small stream of fraudulent data. This attempt at fraud is readily recognized as a perversion of the scientific ethos, but it highlights that there is a moral component to the orientation and

19. Of course, this also means that a scientific culture is subject to a variety of forces not directly related to scientific rationality. They have alliances to people and theories, they can be vain, they may be career oriented, slow to accept new theories, and so on. Hence the process of scientific advance is not linear. See the classic work of Thomas S. Kuhn, *The Structure of Scientific Revolutions*, 2nd ed. (Chicago: University of Chicago Press, 1970), for the ways in which these human factors influence the development of science. Similarly, Lonergan recalls the opinion of Max Planck that "a new scientific position gains general acceptance, not by making opponents change their minds, but by holding its own until old age has retired them from their professorial chairs." See Lonergan, *Insight*, 549.

20. When confronted with the brilliant formulae of the untutored Indian mathematician Srinivasa Ramanujan, the English mathematician G. H. Hardy concluded that they "must be true, because, if they were not true, no one would have the imagination to invent them" (Robert Kanigel, *The Man Who Knew Infinity: A Life of the Genius Ramanujan* [New York: Washington Square Press, 1992], 168). Similarly, when Andrew Wiles published an initial incorrect proof of Fermat's Last Theorem, no one suggested he was being fraudulent—merely mistaken.

skills of the scientist, an orientation to the virtue of honesty. A failure to attend to this virtue can send science down false paths and waste considerable time, money, and intellectual energy.

Again, we may ask what this might teach us about the possibility of proving the existence of God. The differences between scientific and mathematical reasoning might encourage us to examine what other forms of reasoning there might be. Despite its hegemonic claims, there are other valid forms of reasoning besides those of science. Nonetheless, in both mathematics and science, reasoning does lead to questions about existence and nonexistence. The ontological status of the objects of science are perhaps less problematic than those of mathematics, but both revolve around forms of reasoning. As with mathematics, the scientist needs to be trained in certain orientations and skills, including in the case of science certain moral orientations such as honesty. In considering the possibility of proving the existence of God, it may well require of the subject similar orientations and skills for the argument to get traction.

A Metaphysical Paradigm?

We need to consider the question of whether there might be other paradigms of proof apart from mathematics and science that would lead us to affirm the existence of God. Based on our examples above, we might consider the possibility of a community of metaphysicians, with certain well-developed orientations and skills and even appropriate moral dispositions, as a prerequisite to engaging in metaphysics and perhaps then proving God's existence. This would be a reasonable extrapolation to draw from the discussion above. But what would the subject matter of such a form of reasoning be? If science is so successful at dealing with the empirical world, what more is there to say?

Let's begin with science itself. I have made some comments about the scientific method above, and whatever one might think about the accuracy of the account, science lives and dies by its method.[21] Overall, science has more faith in its method than its results, which may be provisional and subject to correction or refinement. What remains constant is the method that is the source of all results, all corrections, and all refinements. However, on what does the validity of the scientific method rest? What proof do we have that the scientific method is valid?

Of course, one cannot use the scientific method to prove the scientific method; that would be circular reasoning. One might take a pragmatic approach and just say, "Who cares? It works well enough." But this is hardly a scientific attitude to such a fundamental question. One cannot simply suppress the question of why the scientific method works so well. Here we return to Einstein's famous comment mentioned in chapter 1, "The most incomprehensible thing about the universe is that it is comprehensible."[22] The universe conforms itself to our scientific method—a method predicated on finding patterns or intelligibility in the empirical data and then verifying that intelligibility through confirming predictions the patterns suggest. We find an alignment between the insights of scientific minds—insights that arise as a product of human intelligence and reason—and the intelligibility of the real world. Why should reality be aligned with mental operations? The underlying question here is the correlation between reason and reality that science assumes as part of its method, but that cannot itself be established by that method.

---

21. Of course, there have been those who reject the notion that science has a "method"; for example, Paul Feyerabend, *Against Method*, ed. Bert Terpstra (Chicago: University of Chicago Press, 1999). But these often take "method" to mean some sort of deductive mechanism that ignores the creative transformative moment of insight and understanding.
22. Albert Einstein, *Ideas and Opinions*, trans. Sonja Bargmann (New York: Bonanza, 1954), 292.

The second observation we can make about the scientific method is the necessity of verifying its theories and hypotheses. Science always needs to test its theories against the empirical evidence. And so, while Einstein postulated that light would bend in a strong gravitational field according to his theory of general relativity, it was Eddington who undertook the scientific experience to verify this prediction. And while Peter Higgs postulated the existence of the Higgs boson in 1965, it was the scientists at the Large Hadron Collider who produced the evidence almost fifty years after the initial prediction. This indicates that scientific theories are not self-verifying. No scientific theory can be so comprehensive, so complete, that it could bypass the necessity of verification in the data. Royal astronomer Martin Rees notes, "Theorists may, some day, be able to write down fundamental equations governing physical reality. But physics can never explain what 'breathes fire' into the equations, and actualizes them in a real cosmos."[23] One can know whether "fire" has been breathed into the equations through empirical verification, but such verification remains, from a scientific perspective, a brute fact. Rees might be surprised if he were told that the distinction he is drawing is nothing less than the Scholastic metaphysical distinction between essence and existence, which is central to the deeper questions of the contingency of the universe.

These two questions, regarding the intelligibility of reality and the necessity of verification, both arise naturally in scientific endeavors as presuppositions of the scientific method. But they are not in themselves scientific issues; rather, they are what we might call "meta-scientific" issues, or what has traditionally been called metaphysics. Metaphysics deals not with this or that empirical reality, as do the sciences, but attempts to say something about the whole—about

---

23. Martin J. Rees, *Just Six Numbers: The Deep Forces that Shape the Universe* (New York: Basic Books, 2000), 131.

truth, existence, and reality. One might then ask whether there exists a community of metaphysicians with certain well-developed orientations and skills, and even appropriate moral dispositions prerequisite to the task of debating questions of reality, existence, and truth, and perhaps even of "proving" God's existence in our current context. Not really, though there are individuals who know something of what is involved. Analytic philosophy, which dominates the Anglo-American world, is only beginning to allow metaphysical questions, having until recently been stuck in questions of ordinary language.[24] Continental philosophy has expressed grave concerns about metaphysics, which it labels "onto-theology," and is burdened with a certain "forgetfulness of being," the fundamental distinction between beings and Being.[25] A small band of neo-Scholastics seek to revive the metaphysical tradition of Thomas Aquinas, but rarely in a way that makes the needed connections with the contemporary context.[26] And even if there were such a community of metaphysicians, what cultural authority would they be able to claim in order to speak of God's existence without a large-scale cultural shift that recognized the validity and shared some of the presuppositions of a metaphysical approach? For most people most of the time, God's existence will be a matter of belief rather than immanently generated knowledge. It will be at best, to again quote Charles Taylor, an "inference . . . at the extreme and most fragile end of a chain of inferences"[27] for anyone without the requisite orientations and skills.[28]

24. For a discussion of this issue, see Andrew Beards, *Method in Metaphysics: Lonergan and the Future of Analytic Philosophy* (Toronto: University of Toronto Press, 2008).
25. See Kevin Hart, *The Trespass of the Sign: Deconstruction, Theology, and Philosophy*, 2nd ed., Perspectives in Continental Philosophy (New York: Fordham University Press, 2000), 75–96.
26. A good exception would be the work of Robert J. Spitzer, *New Proofs for the Existence of God: Contributions of Contemporary Physics and Philosophy* (Grand Rapids: Eerdmans, 2010).
27. Charles Taylor, *A Secular Age* (Cambridge, MA: Belknap, 2007), 558.

A final word on a metaphysical paradigm concerns certain key terms that lie at the heart of the question of God's existence. Consider the three propositions, "X has being," "X exists," and "X is real." Does each proposition assert the same thing about X? The meaning of the key terms *being, existence,* and *reality* are central to any discussion of God's existence, yet they are rarely directly addressed in much of what passes for public debate on the question. In particular, as noted in the previous chapter in relation to Lonergan's proof of the existence of God, for the proof to get traction may require a shift in the meaning of such basic terms. Unreflectively, we may presume that reality is what we touch, see, hear, and so on with our senses. If this is the case, we shall never be able to prove that God is real, because God is not available for sensory inspection. Then to "save" the situation we might seek to distinguish between being "real" and "existing," as if some things are real but don't exist, or exist but are not real. At the heart of this confusion lies the question of what Lonergan calls "intellectual conversion," its presence and absence. This conversion requires an alignment or isomorphism between our knowing (truth) and the known (real/being/existence). Such an alignment is implicit in the scientific method but rarely attended to, and will be fundamental in the development of a proper metaphysical paradigm. I shall make this more explicit in the next chapter.

Conclusion

In this chapter, we have explored something of our contemporary context within which a natural theology needs to operate. We have

---

28. This is not to say there are no works that deal with the question of metaphysics. See, for example, *The Oxford Handbook of Metaphysics*, ed. M. J. Loux and D. W. Zimmerman (Oxford/New York: Oxford University Press, 2003).

considered questions of how reason and proof might operate in relation to the God question by considering the possibility of a metaphysical paradigm of reasoning and perhaps proving God's existence. In one sense, the goal of the chapter was to establish just what can and cannot be done within this context and the need to begin to shift that context as part of the overall project of natural theology. A metaphysical paradigm is an emerging reality, not an existing one, and part of the purpose of this book is to assist in its emergence.

3

Intellect, Reason, and Reality

The Beginning of Intellectual Conversion

In the previous chapter, I considered two accepted contemporary paradigms for knowing and proving (mathematics and science), noted their similarities and differences, and proposed a third paradigm, a metaphysical paradigm, more as a heuristic anticipation rather than an existing fact. In particular, I suggested that Lonergan's notion of intellectual conversion is the key issue in the development of any such metaphysical paradigm. Without it, or something very much like it, it is almost impossible to untangle any real distinction between physics and metaphysics.

In this chapter, we shall explore this issue further, tracing a number of issues that arise in contemporary discussions on science and the efforts of various authors to eliminate God from an account of the origins of the universe. Underlying these efforts is what I call anxiety over contingency—an intellectual anxiety that arises from the very incompleteness of the scientific project. This will be illustrated by reference to the recent work of Lawrence Krauss and his efforts to do for cosmology what Darwin did for biology in eliminating the need for God as an explanatory cause.[1] Krauss is an established physicist who came to public attention with his debunking of some of the "science" behind the Star Trek series.[2] More recently, he has joined forces with the new atheists in claiming that science eliminates the need for God. The muddle that Krauss's most recent work illustrates will help bring us to a fuller account of the issue of intellectual conversion and a recovery of the significance of intelligence and reason in relation to reality.

Science: Hypothetical and Existentially Incomplete

Let us return to the observations made at the conclusion of the previous chapter regarding the nature of scientific discovery and progress. I shall fill out that discussion with a fuller account of the recent discovery of the Higgs boson, its context, and implications.

Peter Higgs first postulated the existence of the Higgs boson in 1965. That postulate formed part of what has become known as the Standard Model in modern physics, a theory that sought to unite in a single account the electromagnetic, weak, and strong interactions between subatomic particles.[3] These are three of the four basic forces in nature, the other being gravitation. This model operates on the basis of identifying underlying symmetries in the known data on these particles and their interactions. Indeed, the notion of symmetry is one of the fundamental unifying notions in modern physics. In

---

1. This is how Richard Dawkins describes Krauss's achievement in the appendix to Lawrence Krauss, *A Universe from Nothing: Why There Is Something Rather Than Nothing* (New York: Free Press, 2012), 191.
2. Lawrence Krauss, *The Physics of Star Trek* (New York: Basic Books, 1995).
3. For an account of the Standard Model, see Robert Oerter, *The Theory of Almost Everything: The Standard Model, the Unsung Triumph of Modern Physics* (New York: Penguin, 2006), written before the discovery of the Higgs boson.

this case, the different particles and fields become related through processes of "symmetry breaking." Prior to this process, the various forces are unified and indistinguishable; after this symmetry breaking, they become distinct but related through symmetry operations. The various particles are then related through these symmetry operations. These operations reveal the deep patterning or intelligibility of subatomic particles.

Theories like the Standard Model are of interest not just when they render existing data intelligible, but when they lead to predictions of new phenomena. The Standard Model made three such predictions: the W and Z bosons, which were discovered in 1981,[4] and the Higgs boson, discovered in 2012. One of the reasons it took so long to discover this predicted particle is the mass of the Higgs boson. The model predicted a mass equivalent to about two hundred protons, or about the mass of a gold nucleus. This is massive for a "subatomic" particle. To produce a particle of such mass required enormous amounts of energy (recalling the relationship between mass and energy proved by Einstein in his famous equation $E = mc^2$). Perhaps the main reason for building the Large Hadron Collider at the CERN facility in Switzerland, one of the largest and most expensive scientific instruments ever built, was to test the Standard Model and prove or disprove the existence of the Higgs boson. It could achieve the needed energy levels.

In the end, the discovery demonstrated that the deep patterning identified by the Standard Model was present and its prediction of the Higgs boson was correct. In fact, the match between theory and experiment is stunning. One physicist blogger, Adam Falkowski, who was working at the CERN at the time, notes that

4. Abdus Salam, Sheldon Glashow, and Steven Weinberg were awarded the Nobel Prize in Physics in 1979 for the theoretical work leading to this discovery. See ibid., 196.

one cannot help noticing that the data are indecently consistent with the simplest Higgs boson of the Standard Model. Overall, adding the [latest] data improved the consistency, eradicating some of the hints of non-standard behavior we had last year. It's been often stressed that the Higgs boson is the special one, a particle different from all the others, a type of matter never observed before. Yet it appears in front of us exactly as described in detail over the last 40 years. This is a great triumph of particle theory.[5]

The universe did not disappoint, but yet again demonstrated its deep intelligibility. The pure intelligibility that arises from complex mathematical theories resonates with what exists in reality.

What would have happened if the scientists had not found the Higgs boson and the Standard Model was not verified? The response would *not* have been, "Well, why should we expect the universe to fit our mathematical models?" Rather, it would have been, "We'll go back to the drawing board and develop new models to test."[6] The scientific drive to understand presumes rather than proves that the material world is intelligible. The continued success of science is a testament to the fact that this presumption is well-founded. We would be astonished if anyone were to suggest anything else. It would be drawing an arbitrary end to scientific investigation.

This discovery also illustrates, as noted in the previous chapter, the ever-present gap between theory and verification. The Standard Model was enormously successful in its account of the basic particles and the forces through which they interact. It was mathematically satisfying and elegantly based on notions of physical symmetry. Yet no one would have suggested that it must be correct regardless of any process of empirical verification. This process lies at the heart of the scientific method. Theories propose, empirical data dispose

---

5. See his blog entry "H-day: the morning after," Monday, July 23, 2012, at http://resonaances.blogspot.com/.
6. In fact, there were already-existing alternate accounts, which now are likely to be shelved for the time being.

(or confirm). Theories are not self-verifying but always remain hypothetical constructs, subject to the next round of verification or falsification from the data.

This leads to a significant tension in the whole scientific project. Its drive is to seek intelligibility or patterns in the empirical data, to express these patterns in theoretical constructs. Yet in the end, it must deal with the brute fact of existence, which either verifies or falsifies these proposed patterns through reference to the data. That reality is intelligible is the presupposition of all scientific endeavors; that the intelligibility science proposes is always subject to empirical verification means that science never actually explains existence itself but must be checked against the empirical data, leading to a "yes" or "no" that confirms or rejects the proposed intelligibility. This existential[7] gap between scientific hypotheses and empirical verified judgment points to, in philosophical terms, the contingency of existence. There is no automatic leap from hypothesis to reality that can bypass a "reality check."

Anxiety over Contingency:
The Multiverse and a "Theory of Everything"

It is not difficult to identify a certain level of intellectual anxiety over this feature of contingency, especially where there may be a suggestion that God is required to overcome the existential gap between hypothesis and verification (in metaphysical terms, between essence and existence).[8] Various claims have been made that

---

7. I use the word "existential" here not in the sense of existential philosophy, which is concerned with issues of personal authenticity and ethical performance, but to describe the question of the existence as distinct from the intelligibility of reality.
8. In simple terms, essence is concerned with *what* a thing is, while existence is concerned with *whether* a thing is. There have been constant debates over whether there is a real distinction between essence and existence, which parallels debates over whether existence is a predicate (or

somehow science can come up with a theory so good it must be true, a "theory of everything" in which all the loose ends are tied up, no free variables remain, and the universe "must" be as the theory predicts. The two main contenders for a solution to the problem of contingency are theories of the multiverse and theories of quantum gravitation. These are not unrelated, but they have distinctive features.

Theories of the "multiverse" arose, at least in part, in response to the work of some scientists on what is called the anthropic cosmological principle.[9] These scientists point out the high degree of fine-tuning present in the universe, making it a suitable place for the emergence of life. They note, for example, the fine balance between the expansive and contractive forces in the Big Bang, ensuring that the universe did not fly apart too quickly, or contract too quickly, for life to emerge.[10] This is an observation of the contingency of certain facts about our universe that seem to have no deeper intelligibility but make our universe life-producing.[11] One response to this contingency is to posit the existence of other "universes" where the physical laws are different from our own, but would not be life-producing. Our universe would then just be a statistical accident among all the possible universes that exist. Various proposals are then put forward for mechanisms to produce all these universes, from the Big Bang to some similar event or process. Then, as Krauss states, physics becomes an "environmental science," the science of our particular cosmic environment.[12]

property) of things. On the position above, there is a real distinction between hypothesis and verification, and hence a real distinction between essence and existence.

9. John D. Barrow and Frank J. Tipler, *The Anthropic Cosmological Principle* (Oxford: Oxford University Press, 1988).

10. There are countless examples of such fine-tuning presented in Barrow and Tipler's book. While such examples are conducive to a theistic account of creation, they are not definitive.

11. In that sense, arguments from the anthropic principle are a form of "argument from design."

12. Krauss, *A Universe from Nothing*, 176.

The multiverse displaces any need for a creator God, since in some sense it is claimed to be self-explanatory.

> The possibility that our universe is one of a large, even possibly infinite set of distinct and causally separated universes, in each of which any number of fundamental aspects of physical reality may be different opens up a vast new possibility for understanding our existence.[13]

The multiverse contains all possible worlds within itself. Krauss writes that "the question of what determined the laws of nature that allowed our universe to form and evolve now becomes less significant. If the laws of nature are themselves stochastic and random, then there is no prescribed 'cause' for our universe."[14]

However, the problem is that the various universes that constitute the multiverse are "causally disconnected", as Krauss notes on three occasions.[15] In fact, they have "always been and always will be causally disconnected from ours,"[16] which implies that we can have no empirical knowledge of their existence. They remain forever empirically unverifiable. So in order to overcome anxiety about contingency, Krauss and others who propose the multiverse are willing to ditch a fundamental aspect of the scientific method: the demand for empirical verification. Of course, one might suggest that the notion of "causal disconnection" should be taken more loosely, and perhaps the theory of a multiverse could be empirically verified. In this case, we are back to the issue of contingency that the multiverse sought to overcome.

Similar observations could be made about claims of a possible future "theory of everything" in which all physical constants are determined uniquely, making it so that there can be only one possible

---

13. Ibid., 176.
14. Ibid., 177.
15. Ibid., 127, 130, 176.
16. Ibid., 127.

universe, uniquely determined by "one big equation." Such a theory would unite the four forces of nature in one account of quantum gravity.[17] These two approaches to overcoming anxiety over contingency intersect when the "one big equation" is used to generate not just this universe, but the whole multiverse. In both cases, we run into the same problem: either such a theory needs to be empirically verified (which again gives rise to contingency) or it seeks to go beyond a fundamental aspect of the scientific method, which requires empirical verification. Indeed, Krauss goes so far as to state that "anything that is not proscribed by the laws of physics *must* actually happen" [emphasis added].[18] This claim is no longer a scientific claim, but a metaphysical one, relieving science from the need for empirical verification altogether.

In metaphysical terms, both the theory of a multiverse and the "theory of everything" are seeking to move beyond contingency to necessity, to formulate what would in traditional terms be called "necessary" being, or being whose existence requires no further explanation. This approach is an attempt to bypass the traditional response, which would identify such a necessary being with God. *But the simple fact is that no mathematical formula creates anything.* In itself, it is the creation of the mind that conceives it. It may help explain what exists, but it does not create the thing it explains. The anxiety over contingency is nonetheless a valid anxiety, because without some necessary being such as God, the drive toward the intelligibility of the universe, the foundational drive of science, hits a brick wall with existence itself. Existence remains radically unintelligible, without

17. The most common popularized account is "string theory," which seeks to unite all forces and particles in a ten- or eleven-dimensional model of space-time. See Brian Greene, *The Elegant Universe: Superstrings, Hidden Dimensions, and the Quest for the Ultimate Theory* (London: Jonathan Cape, 1999), for an account. Interestingly, Krauss is critical of string theory because it has made no verifiable physical claims. See Krauss, *A Universe from Nothing*, 132.

18. Krauss, *A Universe from Nothing*, 165.

explanation, unless it is related in some way to necessary being. If anything, these two failed attempts to bypass the problem of contingency simply reinforce the realization that science is existentially incomplete. We come back to the observation of Martin Rees, noted in the previous chapter: "Theorists may, some day, be able to write down fundamental equations governing physical reality. But physics can never explain what 'breathes fire' into the equations, and actualizes them in a real cosmos."[19] Whatever it is that "breathes fire" can only be a necessary being, an existence that needs no further explanation. As Aquinas would say, "This all people call God."

This, of course, is not a proof that such a being exists, but it does indicate why the notion of a divine being arises in relation to the problem of contingency. It also indicates the vacuous nature of the question, "Who made God?" Necessary being is self-explanatory; it needs no further explanation, no "maker" to explain it. That this question is so regularly trotted out by atheists attacking religious belief underscores how shallow much of their stance actually is. It also shows why God's existence or nonexistence can never be a scientific question. Scientific method is predicated on the need for empirical verification, which means it can only deal with contingent being, not necessary being. We can never get to God as the conclusion of a scientific argument.

Krauss's Metaphysical Muddle

We can observe further confusion in Krauss's approach when he presses his argument that the universe is self-explanatory. As the title of his book, *A Universe from Nothing*, suggests, he claims that science is well on the way to explaining how the universe emerges from

---

19. Martin J. Rees, *Just Six Numbers: The Deep Forces that Shape the Universe* (New York: Basic Books, 2000), 131.

"nothing," thus eliminating any need for a creator God.[20] As Krauss notes, much hangs on what we mean by "nothing." His regular barbs at philosophers and theologians refer to their alleged imprecision in regard to the meaning of "nothing." He, on the other hand, has a perfectly clear understanding of what he means by "nothing." As he repeats often enough to be a mantra, "nothing" means "empty space." Indeed, "'Nothing' is every bit as physical as 'something', especially if it is to be defined as the 'absence of something.'"[21] The failure of philosophers and theologians to realize this indicates the "intellectual bankruptcy" of "much of modern theology and some modern philosophy."[22] He explains, "By *nothing* I do not mean nothing, but rather *nothing*—in this case, the nothingness we normally call empty space."[23]

What comes through time and time again is that real things are things "in" space and time, subatomic particles, even virtual particles, electromagnetic and gravitational fields, and so on. Indeed, I do not dispute the reality of any of these, even virtual particles.[24] But one may ask about the reality of space itself. Is space "real," and does it constitute "something" rather than "nothing"? If space is indeed "something" then Krauss's argument that something comes from nothing ("empty space") is itself empty. Indeed, even he admits, "I assume space exists," so it is clearly not nothing.[25]

Much of Krauss's energy is expended telling us that "nothing [i.e., empty space] is not nothing" at all,[26] but a seething undercurrent

20. Krauss, *A Universe from Nothing.*
21. Ibid., xiv.
22. Ibid., xiv.
23. Ibid., 59.
24. Virtual particles are predicted by quantum mechanics; they can come into and out of existence for short time spans without violating the convservation of energy, due to quantum uncertainty. Their existence has been empirically verified in the Casimir effect. For details, see Stephen Reucroft and John Swain, "What is the Casimir Effect?" http://www.scientificamerican.com/article.cfm?id=what-is-the-casimir-effec.
25. Krauss, *A Universe from Nothing*, 150.

of virtual particles that can "pop" into real existence through their interaction with powerful fields, something Stephen Hawking proved in relation to the gravitation field around black holes in the 1970s.[27] Scientifically, this may well be correct, but it does not address the question of whether something can come from nothing. It merely tells us how some things can come from something else (that is, from empty space, which is not really empty at all).

We can witness here a basic confusion in Krauss's conception of "nothing." Nothing is not defined as the absence of existence or being, but as the emptiness of space and time. But at the same time, space "exists." The ontological status of space is thus confused for Krauss. On the one hand, existence (being "something") occurs within space; on the other hand, space exists. Because space is actually never empty, even "nothing" is something. Krauss is in a metaphysical muddle, but seems completely unaware of the fact. Neither are those who endorse his work such as Sam Harris (who declares it a "brilliant and disarming book") or A. C. Grayling (who claims it is a "triumph of science over metaphysics, reason and enquiry over obfuscation and myth, made plain for all to see"). In an appendix to the book, Richard Dawkins compares it with Darwin's *Origin of Species*, doing for cosmology what Darwin's work did for biology in eliminating the need for God.[28] If nothing else, this demonstrates that it is apparently not just religious thinkers who can suspend the power of critical thought when it suits them.

26. As the title of chapter 9 states, "nothing is something" (ibid., 142).
27. Ibid., 156. The original article was Stephen Hawking, "Black Hole Explosions?" *Nature* 248 (March 1, 1974): 30–31.
28. Krauss, *A Universe from Nothing*, 191.

The Need for Intellectual Conversion:
The Example of Augustine

Krauss's problem is one that is not new to the Christian tradition. Augustine identifies himself as falling into the same problem prior to his conversion to Christianity, and indeed it was a major impediment to that conversion. Augustine begins Book 7 of *The Confessions* with a clear signal as to the main issue he wishes to address in the subsequent material. In its opening paragraph, he draws attention to his major intellectual difficulty in coming to faith: "I was unable to grasp the idea of substance except as something we can see with our bodily eyes" (7.1.1).[29] This had a particular impact on Augustine's ability to conceive of God as other than a body: "I was still forced to imagine something corporeal spread out in space, whether infused into the world or even diffused through the infinity outside it . . . because anything to which I denied these spatial dimensions seemed to me to be nothing at all" (7.1.1).[30] Augustine reinforces this conception of God in a subsequent passage:

> Hence I thought that even you, Life of my life, were a vast reality spread throughout space in every direction: I thought that you penetrated the whole mass of the earth and the immense, unbounded spaces beyond it on all sides, that earth, sky, and all things were full of you, and that they found their limits in you, while you yourself had no limit anywhere. (7.1.2)[31]

In terms Lonergan develops in his major work, *Insight*, both the young Augustine and Krauss are caught in a notion of reality as "already-out-there-now," a reality conditioned by space and time.[32]

---

29. Augustine, *The Confessions*, trans. Maria Boulding (New York: Vintage Books, 1998), 158.

30. Ibid., 159.

31. Ibid., 159.

32. Bernard J. F. Lonergan, *Insight: A Study of Human Understanding*, ed. Crowe Frederick E. and Robert M. Doran, Collected Works of Bernard Lonergan 3 (Toronto: University of Toronto Press, 1992), 276–77.

Lonergan refers to this conception of reality as based on an "animal" knowing, on extroverted, biologically dominated consciousness. He distinguishes it from a fully human knowing based on intelligence and reason, arguing that many philosophical difficulties arise because of a failure to distinguish between these two forms of knowing. This distinction can help us identify why Krauss is confused about the ontological status of space. Our "animal" knowing identifies "reality" as an "already-out-there-now" of things, particles, fields, and so on, "in" space and time. Our genuine fully human knowing, on the other hand, knows that space exists because it is intelligent and reasonable to affirm its reality.

Unlike Krauss, Augustine makes a transition from one position to the other. Indeed, Book 7 of *The Confessions* is the narrative on that transition. Augustine begins the narrative with a conversation with his friend Nebridius concerning the Manichaean belief in a cosmic conflict between powers of darkness and God. Nebridius raises the question, "What would they have done to you [God] if you had refused to fight?" (7.2.3).[33] In raising this question, he shows that no possible answer makes any sense; they are all equally unreasonable. However, from the point of view of the unfolding argument within the narrative, what Augustine presents is an alternative criterion for reality from his previously identified naïve position. Nebridius presents to Augustine a reasoned argument against the Manichaeans. He demonstrates through argument that their position is rationally incoherent, and so the realities they posit are nothing but fables and myths. Rather than the criterion of an extroverted consciousness—which focuses on what is "out there" for inspection—leading the way, the argument of Nebridius turns our attention to a reality based on reason. Later on in Book 7 this

33. Augustine, *The Confessions*, 160.

transition will be realized in Augustine through his reading of the "Platonists," who mediate a shift from materiality as a criterion of reality to a more "spiritual" understanding of reality.[34] Rather than taking materiality as the paradigm for what is real, platonic doctrine views materiality as more ephemeral, more insubstantial, than the reality of truth grasped intellectually. Through his reading of the Platonists, the shift foreshadowed in the juxtaposition of his fixation on corporeality with the reasoned argument of Nebridius begins to take possession of his own thinking.

And so Augustine still talks about light, but now it is an "incommutable light . . . not this common [visible] light at all, but something different, utterly different. . . . Anyone who knows truth knows it, and whoever knows it knows eternity. . . . Love knows it" (7.10.16).[35] God is then referred to as "eternal Truth," whose reality cannot be doubted. "Is truth then a nothing, simply because it is not spread out through space, either finite or infinite?" The reality of truth is now as real to Augustine as his own existence: "No possibility of doubt remained in me; I could more easily have doubted that I was alive than that truth exists, truth that is seen and understood through things that are made" (7.10.16).[36]

Much here depends on how one reads the conjunction "and." Is Augustine positing here two truths: one seen, the other understood? Or is there one truth that is "seen and understood" through created reality? Clearly, the direction Augustine is taking his readers in is the latter rather than the former. Indeed, in a complete inversion of our normal orientation to the "already-out-there-now" real, God is what

---

34. There is much dispute over the exact identity of these Platonists and the extent of Augustine's knowledge of them. See Brian Dobell, *Augustine's Intellectual Conversion: The Journey from Platonism to Christianity* (Cambridge: Cambridge University Press, 2009), for some of the details.

35. Augustine, *The Confessions*, 172–73.

36. Ibid., 173.

is most real, while created material realities "do not in the fullest sense exist . . . they are real because they are from you, but unreal inasmuch as they are not what you are" (7.11.17).[37]

Reclaiming Insight and Judgment

As a scientist, Krauss is of course fully committed to the use of intelligence and reason. Indeed, the whole of the scientific method is predicated on the use of intelligence and reason. Intelligence is the creative ecstatic origin of all scientific hypotheses. The moment of insight—when we move from struggling to grasp anything at all to that moment of illumination when everything becomes clear—is the beginning of every scientific and mathematical discovery. It is Archimedes running naked down the streets of Syracuse calling out "Eureka!"; or Friedrich August Kekulé daydreaming of a snake swallowing its tail and awaking to grasp the cyclic structure of benzene; or Henri Poincaré struggling with the theory of Fuchsian functions, only to have it all fall into place in a flash of insight.[38] Examples could be multiplied in the history of science and mathematics. Large or small, insight marks the beginning of knowledge, the first step from mere gaping to genuine human knowledge.

Nonetheless, it is only a first step. While we well remember the scientific and mathematical successes, the insights that were genuine

---

37. Ibid., 174.

38. He describes the process as follows: "For fifteen days I strove to prove that there could not be any functions like those I have since called Fuchsian functions. I was then very ignorant; every day I seated myself at my work table, stayed an hour or two, tried a great number of combinations and reached no results. One evening, contrary to my custom, I drank black coffee and could not sleep. Ideas rose in crowds; I felt them collide until pairs interlocked, so to speak, making a stable combination. By the next morning I had established the existence of a class of Fuchsian functions, those which come from the hypergeometric series; I had only to write out the results, which took but a few hours." See Arthur Koestler, *The Act of Creation* (London: Hutchinson, 1976), 114–15.

breakthroughs, we tend to forget the less successful ones, the failures, the discarded hypotheses such as "bodily humors" in medicine, or phlogiston to explain combustion, or Descartes's eddies in space to explain planetary motion. They too involved insights, but as Lonergan notes, insights are a dime a dozen. Something more is needed: in science it is verification, and in mathematics it is rigorous proof. Both these involve a movement from insight to judgment, from hypothesis to checking that the hypothesis works or is correct. Insights help us answer "what" questions: what happened, why did it happen, how/when/where did it happen, what is it, why is it so? Judgments, on the other hand, ask, "Is it so?" and result in a yes, or no, or probably/possibly.

This process of reasoning leading to judgment is very different from the process of insight; it is less exciting and more imperious, demanding, and exacting. Alternate explanations need to be eliminated; hidden assumptions need to be uncovered; more data may need to be found; possible predictions or consequences need to be investigated, and so on. This is a process of reasoning; more than just logic and much more than just a mechanical process, it involves an element of personal responsibility. We "sit" in judgment. Our insights are spontaneous and serendipitous; they cannot be forced or produced at will. Judgments involve us as persons, for we may judge too hastily and appear foolish, or too slowly and appear pedestrian. The scientists at CERN had to wait until the moment was right: some would have gone public earlier but run the risk of being proven wrong; others would have delayed and would have appeared overly cautious. Even in mathematics, this process of judgment cannot be trapped into a mechanical process. Andrew Wiles made an initial claim regarding the proof of Fermat's Last Theorem, only to withdraw it when a flaw was identified. More cautious the second time, he checked it with various colleagues before going public with the first accepted proof.[39]

So Krauss is very familiar with the operations of intelligence and reason. However, he and the young Augustine, and most people most of the time, conceive of reality not as uncovered by the operations of intelligence and reason, but by looking. It is the already-out-there-now "real" of animal extroversion. To break out of their metaphysical muddle, Krauss and others need to shift their method for understanding reality from "taking a look" to "intelligently grasping and reasonably affirming." This is the underlying criterion that grounds the scientific method, with hypotheses intelligently grasped and reasonably affirmed in empirical verification. It is not an alien intrusion into the scientific project, but it is nonetheless a startling and unsettling shift to accomplish. Indeed, it is so startling that if you do not think it is startling, you haven't made it. This shift is the beginning of what Lonergan calls "intellectual conversion."

A Zen Koan

To capture something of the startling nature of the shift, we can consider the ancient Zen koan, "First there is a mountain, then there is no mountain, then there is a mountain again." Let us take each section in turn.

First there is a mountain. On the naïve view, we know the mountain by looking. We open our eyes and it's there. What more is there to say? Our sense of reality is determined by animal extroversion, by the operations of our senses. This "reality" has a solidity to it, an indubitable quality, until it is unsettled by philosophical questions

---

39. For details, see Simon Singh, *Fermat's Last Theorem: The Story of a Riddle that Confounded the World's Greatest Minds for 358 Years* (London: Fourth Estate, 1998).

about the reliability of sense data and *Matrix*-like suggestions of computer simulations.

Then there is no mountain. The first thing that happens when one shifts to this new criterion for reality is that the "reality" of the already-out-there-now "real" of animal extroversion suddenly seems less real, less solid. Like Plato, one begins to distinguish between the appearance and the reality, or with Kant between the phenomena and the noumena. In Plato's myth of the cave, the world of the senses becomes just a shadowy reflection of the real world of ideas. The mountain known by looking is no longer "really real," but just a shadow. In fact, idealist philosophers tend to get stuck at the "there is no mountain" phase because they neglect the role of judgment in the process of knowing. Still, the act of judgment pushes us further into human subjectivity and personal responsibility, not away from it, which can be even more unsettling.

Then there is a mountain again. Through judgment we return to the "reality" of the mountain, a reality of intelligent grasping and reasonable affirmation. It may be a commonsense judgment that grasps the meaning of the word "mountain" and makes a reasonable judgment that the thing towering over the horizon is in fact a mountain. Or it may be the judgment of a geologist who grasps the forces that lead to the formation of mountains and can identify in the prevailing geology those forces at work to produce this particular mountain, again leading to the judgment that this is in fact a mountain. Or it may be the judgment of a surveyor whose rule book specifies that mountains are of a certain height, and this one fits the criterion, so it is a mountain.[40]

---

40. This is a reference to the film *The Englishman Who Went Up a Hill But Came Down a Mountain*, in which a surveyor finds that what he had thought to be a hill has sufficient height to be reclassified as a mountain. The shift in height is, however, a matter of subterfuge from the locals, who want it to be classified as a mountain.

The importance of the shift is thus not that it eliminates things from our list of what is real. The mountains are still really mountains. But it changes the criteria by which we recognize their reality. And in doing so, it opens up the possibility of other things being real that are not present to our already-out-there-now animal extroversion.

Welcome to a Fuller Reality

I noted in the first chapter Lonergan's claim that you cannot prove the existence of God to a materialist without first converting the materialist away from materialism. In the present context, if we think of the "real" as the already-out-there-now real of extroverted consciousness, then God is not real. God becomes just a figment of the imagination, a fairy at the bottom of the garden, an invisible friend. However, if the real is constituted by intelligent grasp and reasonable affirmation, then reality suddenly becomes much richer, and the God-question takes on a different hue.

But it is not just the God-question that we can now begin to address more coherently. There is a whole range of other realities whose reality we can now affirm. Often theistic apologists will refer to something like love. Is love between two people "real"? Of course it is. But there are more mundane things as well: interest rates, mortgages, contracts, vows, national constitutions, penal codes, and so on. Where do interest rates "exist"? Not in banks or financial institutions. Are they real when we cannot touch them or see them? We spend so much time worrying about them; in fact, I'm sure we all worry much more about interest rates than about the existence or nonexistence of the Higgs boson! Similarly, a contract is not just a piece of paper, but the meaning the paper embodies; it is the same with a national constitution or a penal code. Once we break the stranglehold on our thinking by our animal extroversion, we can affirm the reality of our whole world of human meanings and values—of institutions, nations, finance and law, of human relationships, and so on—without the necessity of seeing them as "just" something else lower down the chain of being, yet to be determined.

Another important area that opens up for us is the realm of consciousness itself. For the "reality" of animal extroversion, consciousness is a profound mystery. It cannot be touched or tasted, seen or heard, so its reality is truly suspect. It is not "out there" to be inspected and analyzed, so at most it can be assigned the status of epiphenomenon, a secondary phenomenon reflecting some other underlying reality—in this case, brain states. And so our inner life of thought and feeling, of hopes and desires, is reduced to mere shadows of our brain biochemistry. We can avoid such reductionism by intelligently grasping and reasonably affirming the existence of consciousness. We can easily grasp that there is a difference between being in a coma, under anesthetic, or in a dreamless sleep, on the one hand, and dreaming, being awake and alert, understanding something, making a judgment, or coming to a decision, on the other. In the former states (coma, etc.), "I" am not present; I feel and think nothing. In the latter states, I am the subject of those experiences. I am present as the subject of dreaming, alertness, understanding, judging, or deciding. Understanding this difference and affirming its reality is what is meant by being "conscious." We shall explore the significance of this position on consciousness further in the next chapter. This stance also allows us to avoid the mistake of thinking we can inspect consciousness through some "inner look" (an "already-*in*-there-now" real), which is impossible because we cannot "look at the looker." Knowing consciousness is not a matter of looking at it, but attending to the difference between being in a coma or dreamless sleep and being awake and alert.

Affirming the real as intelligible and reasonable also allows us to resist the overpowering reductionism of many scientific claims. While not intrinsic to science per se, scientific explanations are often driven by the claims that a particular phenomenon is "nothing but" a set of underlying states. The approach is a by-product of thinking that reality is already-out-there-now; the closer I look, the more intense my gaze, the more and more detail and the smaller and smaller things I see. Indeed, even when the things we are seeking are so small we shall never actually "see" them in any meaningful sense, we still maintain this myth of knowing. Thus every science is then thought to be just a set of footnotes on the most basic science of all, probably particle physics, which gives us the ultimate "building blocks" of reality.

A good example of this is the claim that chemistry is "nothing but" the quantum physics of the outer-shell electrons of the various elements. Certainly solving Schrödinger's equation for a single electron around a nucleus does provide the basic structure of the various electron shells, at least as a hypothesis. But as far as I know, no one has solved Schrödinger's equation for the lead atom, which has eighty-two electrons in orbit around its nucleus.[41] The perturbation equations are far too complex to solve, so it is presumed that the results will be similar to those of the hydrogen atom.[42] Should chemists hold off the chemical study of lead until the equations are solved? Of course not; the basic terms and relations of chemistry (atomic number and valence) were well understood before quantum mechanics was discovered, once Mendeleev created the periodic table. They constitute a reasonably affirmed intelligibility, knowable

---

41. The example of lead here is fairly arbitrary. One could choose any of the heavier elements.
42. These perturbations arise because the electrons interact with one another through a repulsive electromagnetic force. It is unlikely that the "n-body" quantum problem for this situation can be solved mathematically, but numerical solutions for simple cases can be found.

quite independently of quantum mechanics. Chemistry is a distinct branch of knowledge, not just a subdivision of physics.

In fact, the totalizing claims of such reductionism impinge not just on chemistry but on every discipline. Biology, too, must submit itself to the final judgment of the physicist, as must the psychologist, the economist, the town planner, the sociologist, and so on. Since only physics talks about basic reality and everything is constructed from its building blocks, it alone can make the final and definitive judgment on everything. There is something audacious, arrogant, and outlandish about such a claim. And it is not a scientific claim but a metaphysical claim.[43] Once we allow all systematic disciplines to discover and define their own intelligible patterns, their own basic terms and relations, which can then be empirically tested and verified, we have a genuine reality that is not reducible to what underlies it. It is not just theologians who have cause to reject such reductionism.

The reductionist paradigm also fails even at the subatomic level. We are often told that the nucleus of an atom is comprised of protons and neutrons. This basic model of the atom was developed in the early twentieth century, when protons and neutrons were thought to be basic building blocks of matter. But there is something wrong even with this account. A bare neutron has a half-life of about eleven and a half minutes.[44] Over time, it decays into a proton, an electron, and an antineutrino. However, once inside the nucleus of an atom, this basic property of the neutron ceases to function. Its integration into the higher-order intelligibility of the atomic nucleus changes its properties. The higher-order reality has modified the lower-order constituent. Indeed, if this did not happen there would be no stable atomic nuclei, no stable chemical substances, and we would not exist.

---

43. This is, of course, a variation on the "law of the instrument": if all you have is a hammer, everything looks like a nail. If all you know is physics, everything must be reduced to physics.
44. See http://hyperphysics.phy-astr.gsu.edu/hbase/particles/proton.html.

Perhaps once we recognize this process, it becomes less troubling that the higher-order integration we call consciousness can modify the lower-order properties of the body without becoming the proverbial "ghost in the machine."

There are other issues we shall consider later on in relation to intellectual conversion. They will become important in our discussion of the good, and in relation to the problem of evil. Indeed, I would go so far as to suggest that any attempted "theodicy" or defense of God in relation to the problem of evil stands or falls on the question of intellectual conversion. In the meantime, we should review just what this means about reality. If reality is what we can intelligently grasp and reasonably affirm, then the real world is shot through with intelligibility, because to lack intelligibility is to be unreal, to not exist. And so Nebridius demonstrated to Augustine the unreality of the Manichaean position by showing that it led to unintelligible and unreasonable conclusions. Grasping this connection between reality and intelligibility lies at the heart of Lonergan's proof for the existence of God, which argues that "reality is completely intelligible." Without intellectual conversion, such an assertion looks like nonsense; with intellectual conversion, it starts to become inescapable.

Not Just a Problem for Scientists

To be fair to Krauss, the issue of a lack of intellectual conversion is not just a problem for physicists or the scientific community in general. It is much more widespread, and can also be illustrated in the work of professional philosophers. In the *Oxford Handbook of Metaphysics* we find the following assertion from philosopher Tim Maudlin:

> Metaphysics is the theory of being, that is, the most generic account of what there is. As such it must be informed by empirical science, since we can only discover the nature of the material world through our experience of it. The most general and fundamental account of material reality is provided by physics, hence physics is the scientific discipline most closely allied to (if not continuous with) metaphysics as a philosophical inquiry.[45]

Clearly, such a stance lacks the basics of intellectual conversion. It demonstrates all the reductionism of the "already-out-there-now" reality of extroverted consciousness, so that in the end it cannot distinguish between metaphysics and physics in any meaningful sense—they are allied, if not continuous. Maudlin presumes what must be proved: that the most generic account of what is—being—is coterminous with empirical reality. Once such a presumption is in place, the whole world of human meanings and values and the consciousness that generates them become very mysterious and, indeed, illusory. Once we break the power of this myth, however, the whole world and its reality are opened up to us.

Conclusion

The focus of this chapter has been the central role of intellectual conversion in any attempt to begin to think metaphysically. Of course, people attempt to think metaphysically without it, but they inevitably end up displaying the type of confusion seen in Krauss's attempt to prove the universe can come from "nothing." One consequence of intellectual conversion is, as we have seen above, to break the hold on our imaginations of the aggressive scientific reductionism that dominates much of the discussion around science

---

45. Tim Maudlin, "Distilling Metaphysics from Quantum Mechanics," in *The Oxford Handbook of Metaphysics*, ed. M. J. Loux and D. W. Zimmerman (Oxford/New York: Oxford University Press, 2003), 461.

and religion. Such a reductionism is a metaphysical stance, one not "proven" by science, and in fact one that runs counter to a scientific commitment to intelligence (hypothesis formation) and reason (verification). Once we move from a conception of reality as already-out-there-now to one where reality is uncovered through intelligent grasp and reasonable affirmation, reductionism loses its force. Further, we are able to affirm the reality of our human world of meanings and values without seeing them as just "nothing more than" some underlying, more "real," reality.

Intellectual conversion is the beginning of a needed therapeutic recovery of the true nature of reason. To lack intellectual conversion is not to be unintelligent or to be operating in bad faith; it is simply a matter of not yet having the requisite intellectual orientation needed to think metaphysically. It is not necessary in order to believe in the existence of God, but it may be necessary if one wishes to provide an intelligent and reasonable account of God's existence. One of the ironies of the modern situation is that the more successful reason has been in the form of scientific reason, the more some have sought to limit it to this sphere of reason alone. Disciplines that are not "scientific" are then deemed to be mere works of fiction. However, reason cannot be constrained in such a straitjacket. The full scope of reason is the universe of being proportionate to our knowing. The key question for natural theology is the possibility of inferring the existence of a being who transcends the proportionality of our knowing, whose existence we can affirm without understanding what exactly that being might be. As Aquinas would say, we seek to know that God exists, not what God is.

4

———

Consciousness, Spirit, and God

As I have argued in this work, natural theology always has a context, a cultural setting within which it seeks to operate. One of the major issues facing a contemporary natural theology is the question of subjectivity/consciousness/self-awareness that was raised in the previous chapter.[1] Here we face a paradoxical situation, in which scientific reductionist accounts of consciousness want to reduce it to a mere epiphenomenon, reflective of lower-order brain states. Indeed, this reductionism pervades all claims to the "objectivity" of science, as if science itself occurs independent of the subjectivity of the scientists who produce it. Subjectivity is written out of the equation. On the other hand, in the development of modern philosophy since the time of Descartes, questions of human subjectivity and consciousness have been central. As Charles Taylor has documented, philosophers have

---

1. See, for example, J. P. Moreland, "The Argument from Consciousness," in *The Blackwell Companion to Natural Theology*, ed. William Lane Craig and J. P. Moreland (Oxford: Blackwell, 2009), 282–343.

assisted in the development of a rich and varied account of human subjectivity in the fields of cognitional and ethical reflection.[2]

However, there have been two major problems with this turn to subjectivity. The first, beginning with Descartes, is the problem of a dualism that separates "mind" from "body," leading to the notion of mind as a sort of "ghost in the machine." This gives rise to the false problem of how, then, the mind can bridge the gap between materiality and spirit in order to affect the physical universe.[3] The second, related problem works the other way, and is perhaps most prominent in Kant. It is the problem of how we get the outside, inside. How can we be sure that the operations of the mind have anything at all to do with the real world? How do we bridge the gap between the object to be known and the subject who knows? This false epistemological problem leads in the end to subjectivism, relativism, and skepticism.

However, in the account developed here, where reality is known through intelligence and reason, making the distinction between inner and outer worlds is itself the product of intelligence and reason. It is not something given immediately in the data itself. One does not need to build an epistemological bridge between object and subject; one instead builds a moat in learning to make the proper distinction between the data of consciousness and the data of sense.

These issues are relevant to the project of natural theology. If we are going to conceive of God with any degree of sophistication, we are going to think of God as a personal being—personal not in the sense of some old man in the clouds, but as one who knows and wills. In seeking to find analogies for God's existence, then, we

---

2. Charles Taylor, *Sources of the Self: The Making of the Modern Identity* (Cambridge, MA: Harvard University Press, 1989); Taylor, *A Secular Age* (Cambridge, MA: Belknap, 2007).

3. See Moreland, "The Argument from Consciousness." Much of this essay is concerned with the issue of the emergence of consciousness and how consciousness can be thought of as affecting the physical world.

will probably turn to the only beings we know who "know and will": ourselves. But to know ourselves as knowers and willers is to know ourselves as conscious beings, because these are operations we simply do not perform when we are unconscious—for example, when in a coma. Mistakes we make in facing the problems of modern discussions about consciousness and subjectivity will then reflect back on our understandings of what it might mean to talk about God's existence.

Thus the purpose of this chapter is to open up the question of consciousness and explore its significance and consequences. To do so will require the introduction of a basic distinction. This distinction helps clarify what is being argued, and also helps familiarize readers with their own experience of consciousness, its operations, and the significance of those operations. As we shall see, these are not necessarily new questions in the history of thought, though some of the illustrations might have more to do with our own context. Once this distinction is in place, we can begin to formulate a more positive, though analogous, notion of what divine existence might be like and why we might affirm such an existence.

Consciousness: A Basic Distinction

The use of the term "consciousness" is often ambiguous—so much so that discussion of consciousness is often confused and meaningless. People will use terms such as *consciousness, self-consciousness, awareness, self-awareness, subjectivity,* and so on as if their meanings are clear and transparent, when in fact commonsense language confuses and conflates various distinct realities.

We shall begin, then, with a basic distinction between consciousness and unconsciousness that was introduced in the previous chapter. We recognize the state of being unconscious: we are unresponsive to gentle sensory stimulation; we do not think, feel, see, or hear. Patients under anesthesia can awake from an operation with little or no experience of the passing of time. While I may be present in body, I am not present in mind: I am unconscious. To be conscious, then, is not to be unconscious. I become the subject of thought and feeling, of seeing and hearing. I am aware of the passing of time, am present not just in body but in mind, and so on. This distinction leads to a number of observations.

First, these experiences correlate with certain activities within the brain. Such activities can be measured on instruments such as an electroencephalogram (EEG), and may well tell us on their own whether the subject is conscious or not. But the subject does not need an EEG to know that she is conscious; she can know that she is conscious simply by attending to the distinctions above. Indeed, her being conscious is the condition for the possibility of her knowing anything at all. Just as a chemist can understand and verify the intelligibility of the periodic table without reference to the discoveries of quantum mechanics, so too the subject can understand and verify her own conscious operations without any reference to brain states. The reductionism of some modern approaches to consciousness does not do full justice to the reality.

Second, consciousness is an "emergent" property. It is not present when we are unconscious; we awake and emerge into consciousness. This happens every day for most of us. We are not constantly conscious; we spend several hours a night in dreamless sleep. However, once we are conscious all our activities change. While unconscious, our hair grows, we digest our food, our heart beats and lungs fill with air: all signs of life. Sadly, some people are permanently in this state, which we refer to as a vegetative state. Higher-order operations are missing. When consciousness emerges, however, everything changes. We orient ourselves to our environment, we feel hungry and thirsty, and so seek food and drink, we avoid unnecessary discomfort and pain, and if we have the time and leisure we think thoughts and dream dreams. Consciousness becomes an organizing principle for a living animal once it emerges. The emergence of consciousness clearly provides a living being with an evolutionary advantage; it allows for a more flexible response to the environment. The conscious animal can seek out and detect its food through sight, hearing, and smell. With taste it can detect more suitable food and water and protect itself from poisonous or harmful material. However, this advantage comes at a price: the very mechanism of consciousness that allows for the refinement of these senses allows for the emergence of pain, the body's warning system that an animal is under threat and must respond to save itself. Pain is the conscious experience of reaching the physical, chemical, biological, and psychological limits of a finite biological being.

Third, on this account of consciousness, non-human animals and human beings both enjoy the property of consciousness. While I do not have direct access to the consciousness of a dog, I can observe the transitions identified above occurring in a dog. They sleep and are unresponsive; they awake and want food and attention. There is enough evidence to suggest that a new organizing principle has emerged and is operating, a principle that was not active in the animal while asleep. Still, I cannot verify consciousness in an animal in the same direct way I can verify it in myself. My access to the consciousness of a dog is indirect.

Fourth, this means that it is not consciousness per se that distinguishes human beings from other members of the animal kingdom.[4] Consciousness itself is a biological fact, an emergent property from underlying physical, chemical, and biochemical conditions. Once we reject the reductionism of the already-out-there-now real, its emergence is no more mysterious than the distinction between chemistry and physics. And as we saw in the previous chapter, higher-order integrations can affect that lower-order substrate, as when the properties of a neutron are changed by being within the nucleus of an atom. What become important for our considerations are the qualities and operations that distinguish human consciousness from that of other animals.

Fifth and finally, it would not be far wrong to suggest that the central distinguishing feature of human consciousness is the drive of intelligence and reason. Human beings are oriented toward meaning and truth (and goodness, but more on that later). This orientation drives mathematics, science, and all our ponderings about the meaning and purpose of life (art, literature, poetry, philosophy, and theology). From whenever we might measure human beginnings—200,000 years ago or perhaps more—to the present, we have moved from primitive hunter-gatherers to landing spacecraft on Mars, from simple cave drawings to the artistic beauty of Monet and Beethoven, from sagas of battle and the hunt to the literary brilliance of Tennessee Williams and Patrick White, from simple counting to solving Fermat's Last Theorem, and from staring at the stars in wonder to discovering the Higgs boson. In a time frame that in evolutionary terms is a mere blink of an eye, we have discovered evolution, decoded the human genome, unleashed the power of the atom, created the most amazing computers, and plumbed the depths of cosmic origins. Intelligence and reason have explosive consequences in science, technology, our social ordering and cultural achievements, and so on. Whatever reductionists might say about human intelligence being not much different from what we see in

4. It is not clear precisely where, if anywhere, the dividing line is within the animal kingdom. It could well be that rudimentary forms of consciousness are present in very primitive animal life forms.

the higher mammals, there is simply no evidence in any other species on the planet of this same explosive quality that has transformed the existence of our human species and the planet, for better or worse.[5] The drive to understand and know the truth of things and give expression to them has defined our existence. This drive is only present in consciousness, for when we are not conscious, intelligence and reason simply do not operate. The emergence of intelligence and reason in human beings clearly gives human beings an evolutionary advantage as well as flexibility in terms of our environmental niche. Rather than being confined to a particular location, human beings have survived in every environment on the planet, from the frigid areas of the Arctic Circle to fiery desert regions, from the highest mountain ranges to technologically assisted living under the sea. Nonetheless, there is a disproportion to the emergence of intelligence and reason that seems to go beyond merely biological imperatives to survive and multiply. There is no clear biological advantage in being able to solve Fermat's Last Theorem, or in discovering the Higgs boson. This disproportion should give some pause to those who give an account of reason that is merely biological in origin.

Know Thyself

The Delphic maxim, "Know thyself," remains as pertinent today as it is unheeded. The dominance of the already-out-there-now

---

5. I recently heard a biologist claim that pigeons can display mathematical ability. Well, in 200,000 years human beings have moved from basic counting to solving Fermat's Last Theorem. In the same time span, what have pigeons (or any other species) achieved? While other animals may display characteristics that are the simulacra of human intelligence, these do not form the central core of those animals' existence and do not drive them to the discoveries of science or the creation of culture. It is rather odd that scientists should expend such enormous amounts of scientific intelligence to make the claim that human intelligence is no different from that of various animals. One might be more convinced if a chimpanzee scientist made the same claims about human intelligence.

orientation of extroverted consciousness means that the inner life of most people is a vast *terra incognita*, an unexplored country filled with the unknown. However, while modern depth psychological approaches and therapeutic movements have made some people more aware of the inner life of affectivity, the inner workings of intelligence and reason often remain hidden. Even when they are explored, they are subject to misconstrual and truncation. For example, as Lonergan quipped in *Insight*, "Empiricism amounts to the assumption that what is obvious in knowing [i.e., looking] is what knowing obviously is."[6] We all understand and know things. But when it comes to having an account of our understanding and knowing, and how they relate to the real and being, we flounder.

In order to know oneself as a knower, one must engage in the activity of knowing—not in an unreflective way but with attentiveness and deliberation. And so, for example, in Plato's dialogue *Meno*, Socrates takes a slave boy through the processes of a mathematical proof to draw out the experience of knowing, not just in the slave boy but more importantly in the reader. The reader is drawn into the experience of coming to the mathematical truth as expounded by Socrates. Likewise, in his study of Christian belief in God as Trinity, *De Trinitate*, Augustine seeks to develop his famous psychological analogy for distinguishing the three persons of the Trinity. However, he recognizes that his readers are not familiar with the techniques of "introspection," so before he can proceed he must provide them with a set of "five-finger exercises" to get them more familiar with their own interiority. Book 8 of *De Trinitate* serves as a general and gentle introduction into the realm of interiority, inviting the reader to reflect on the experience of truth: "Come, hold it in that

---

6. Bernard J. F. Lonergan, *Insight: A Study of Human Understanding*, ed. Frederick E. Crowe and Robert M. Doran, Collected Works of Bernard Lonergan 3 (Toronto: University of Toronto Press, 1992), 441.

first moment in which so to speak you caught a flash … when the word 'truth' was spoken" (8.3).[7] Is Augustine here alluding to the flash of insight? He reminds the readers of their various judgments of value and invites them to explore the interior ground of these judgments (8.4–5). Also, in his monumental study, *Insight*, Lonergan peppers his initial chapters with examples drawn from mathematics and the sciences, drawing out the implications of insight for his readers.[8]

With these precedents in mind, I invite the reader to work through a mathematical example of insight and reasoning, one that I still remember from my first encounter with it as a junior secondary school student (having paper and pen in hand may help the reader in what follows). It is one of the first proofs one encounters in mathematics, alongside geometrical proofs drawn from Euclid: the proof of the irrationality of the square root of two, $\sqrt[2]{2}$. This means that $\sqrt[2]{2}$ cannot be expressed as the ratio of two whole numbers or integers. In the West, this discovery seems to have been first made by the school of Pythagoras, and was such a shocking discovery that they kept it secret. It devastated their hope that all reality could be expressed as ratios of integers.[9] Be that as it may, it is now well-known to any mathematician.

The proof proceeds by way of contradiction. One first assumes that $\sqrt[2]{2}$ is rational and then seeks to achieve some contradiction or unintelligible outcome of that assumption. This is not dissimilar to Nebridius's argument against the Manichaeans: assume their position is correct and derive some outlandish conclusion, thus proving that the initial position must then be false. So one assumes that $\sqrt[2]{2}$ is a

7. Augustine, *The Trinity*, trans. Edmund Hill, ed. John E. Rotelle, OSA (Brooklyn, NY: New City, 1991), 243. The translation by Hill has a flash "from the corner of your eye," which is not in the Latin, and in the context misses the point.
8. Lonergan, *Insight*, chs. 1–4.
9. One legend has it that the person who actually discovered it did so at sea and was promptly thrown overboard.

rational number, that is, the ratio of two whole numbers, **a** and **b**, and one seeks some unintelligible conclusion. Let us assume there are two integers, **a** and **b**, such that:

$$^2\sqrt{2} = a/b \qquad (1)$$

This tells us little, so we remove the offending square root by squaring both sides:

$$2 = (a/b)^2 \qquad (2)$$

And multiplying both sides by b^2 gives us:

$$2b^2 = a^2 \qquad (3)$$

Now we have integers on both sides. Integers are things we are more familiar with, so we might start to get some traction on what to do next. But what do we do next? One can add, divide, multiply, and subtract to one's heart's content, and still be none the wiser. Prior to this, the steps have been relatively mechanical, but now we need an insight—something that focuses on the right observation to make to carry the process forward. But how do we know what the right observation is when we don't know what will or will not carry the process forward? Of course, a trained mathematical mind knows exactly what to do, but only because the needed insight has become so habitual that it no longer breaks in unannounced.

Now, of all the observations we might make based on equation (3) above, one is that a^2 must be an even number since it is equal to $2b^2$. Intelligence grasps that this may be the one relevant fact that will push the argument forward. This is an insight, but one that falls short of a judgment or proof. It is more like an intelligent guess, a possible lead. So if a^2 is even, it is not difficult to conclude that **a** must also be even. Squaring odd numbers gives us an odd number, and squaring even numbers give us an even number. If **a** must be even, then for some integer **c** we would get:

$$a = 2c \qquad (4)$$

But if we substitute (4) into (3) we get:

$$2b^2 = 4c^2 \qquad (5)$$

On dividing both sides by 2, we get:

$$b^2 = 2c^2 \qquad (6)$$

This is just what we had above in (3), only now it is telling us that **b** is also even. This means that for some other integer **d** we can get:

$$b = 2d \qquad (7)$$

Substituting this into (6), then, tells us that:

$$2c^2 = 4d^2 \qquad (8)$$

Or, dividing both sides by 2,

$$c^2 = 2d^2 \qquad (9)$$

Once again, we are back to the same type of equation we had in (3). Again we can conclude that **c** must also be even, or for some integer **e**:

$$c = 2e \qquad (10)$$

This means that:

$$a = 2c = 4e \qquad (11)$$

However, the process does not stop there. We can do the whole thing again and again, finding that not only is **a** divisible by 2, but also by

4, and then by 8, and so on for as many multiples of 2 as we like. And so our assumption that there are integers **a** and **b** leads to the conclusion that **a** (and **b** as well, if one carries through the argument) can be divided by 2 as often as we like and still be an integer. Clearly no positive integer has this property, so no such number exists. The square root of 2 cannot be rational.

Many minds would be happy to rest content with this outcome, but intelligence is restless and can push the matter further. It can seek to generalize the result to other instances. How far can we push the argument above? Is there, for example, anything special about the fact that we took the square root of 2 as our starting point? What if we take the nth root of 2 ($\sqrt[n]{2}$)? A flash of insight would suggest that the proof goes through almost exactly the same. What about the number 2 itself? Why not the square root of 3? Clearly this, too, works just as well with slight modification, but 4 does not. Again, an insight might then suggest that we can replace 2 with any prime number, **p**.[10] With some work (an exercise for the reader), basically the same proof with slight modification follows through. Finally, bringing these two insights together, we can ask about $\sqrt[n]{p}$, and again we grasp that this too will work, leaving the details as a simple extension of what was started in (1) above.

There are two pertinent observations in relation to this mathematical digression. The first is the generativity of insight. Once the initial insight is grasped, it is readily generalized to other examples. Aristotle observed this in his work on the mind, *De Anima*. He contrasted strong sensory input with strong insight. Strong sensory input renders the sense organ temporarily nonreceptive: a strong light blinds the eyes; a strong sound deafens the ears. A

---

10. Recall that a prime number p is one whose sole factors are 1 and p. Of course the proof can work with other numbers than primes, but primes are the easiest cases to push the argument through.

strong insight, on the other hand, opens the mind up to further insights.[11] The mind is not overwhelmed, but gallops forward to explore implications and possibilities. This is an important distinction between the world of sense and the world of understanding.

The second observation concerns the use of the dummy variables, n and p. They refer, respectively, to all natural numbers bigger than 1 and to all primes. Both these sets of numbers are infinite.[12] An insight that grasps that $\sqrt[n]{p}$ is irrational is doubly infinite.[13] The one insight contains all possible cases in a single conscious event. It does not need a distinct insight for each case, piling them up one by one, which would take forever, but grasps all in one go. This should give pause to those who seek a purely materialist explanation for the workings of intelligence. Material systems are by their nature finite combinations and permutations of their underlying components. One insight, on the other hand, can grasp infinite possibilities. Intelligence can generalize from a small number of examples, even just one, to a large, even infinite number of cases.

This is the quality of the intellect that Aristotle spoke of when he called intellect "separable." If intellect is separable from materiality, the question naturally arises as to whether intellect can continue after death, apart from bodiliness. Aristotle himself equivocated on such a possibility, while Aquinas thought it not only possible, but sought to prove it as actually the case. While this is not the place to go

---

11. Aristotle, *De Anima*, 429a, in *The Basic Works of Aristotle*, ed. Richard McKeon, Modern Library Classics (New York: Random House, 2009), 590: "After strong stimulation of a sense we are less able to exercise it than before, as e.g. in the case of a loud sound we cannot hear easily immediately after, or in the case of a bright colour or a powerful odour we cannot see or smell, but in the case of mind, thought about an object that is highly intelligible renders it more and not less able afterwards to think objects that are less intelligible: the reason is that while the faculty of sensation is dependent upon the body, mind is separable from it."
12. Again, the proof that there are an infinite number of primes was well known in the ancient world, and again the reader is invited to consider why it might be true.
13. Of course, this adds nothing to the degree of infinity, but it does add emphasis to the power of insight in this particular case.

into such details, in the context of a natural theology it raises the question of the natural immortality of the soul. While Kant ruled such a conclusion to be beyond the realms of pure reason, his case was based on the phenomena-noumena distinction. This distinction vanishes once intellectual conversion comes into play.

Mind, Spirit, Matter

This property of insight, that it can transcend the limitations of the purely material order, is what is meant in metaphysical terms by calling intellect "spiritual." The word *spiritual* conjures up all sorts of images and expectations. For some, it means the same as or similar to "religious," or some "higher state of consciousness," or perhaps the fantasies of "spiritualism," with spirits referring to ghosts and the like. However, a controlled metaphysical meaning of the term *spiritual* is the nonmaterial: that which is not contained by or limited to materiality. To assert that intellect is spiritual is a direct assault on the dominant materialism of the modern scientific worldview.

I have already argued above for the inadequacy of that worldview. It is based on a view of reality as already-out-there-now and leads to a reductionism that threatens not only theology and philosophy, but all disciplines other than particle physics. If in its place we view the world as uncovered through intelligence and reason, then this reductionism loses its power. We can then affirm not only the distinctiveness of chemistry from physics, but the reality of our human world of meanings and values, of marriage and mortgages, of constitutions and penal codes, and so on. For most people most of the time this is the most real of all worlds, where they are born and mature, go to school, receive an education, learn about science, math, literature, art and culture, learn to become law-abiding citizens, vote in elections, get a job, and perhaps fall in love, marry, and raise a family of their own. When we view reality through the lens of intelligence and reason, we can affirm the reality of this fuller human world without the overpowering reductionism of the scientific worldview.

Indeed, this world demonstrates the fruitfulness and generativity of human intelligence. Many of the things we take for granted in this world of human meaning and value began as ideas. Take democracy, for example. Initially an experiment in ancient Greece, it was built on the idea of the equality of men. At first it included free men, not slaves, and certainly not women. In the more recent history of the West it took shape in bloody struggles with despotic monarchs, but the forms it took in different lands were very different—constitutional monarchies vs. republics, bicameral vs. single houses of parliament, differing electoral systems, and so on. Gradually, the voting franchise was extended from those who owned land to all men, and then to all adult men and women, but generally only after protest and struggle. All these are different instantiations of one basic idea. Insight, judgment, and decision are constitutive of this human world in all its richness, variation, and complexity. They generate the world of technology, economics, politics, and culture.

This world of meaning and value shares some characteristics with the "spirituality" of insight. It sits loosely in relation to materiality. For example, where does the constitution of a nation reside? In its founding document? Yes and no. The actual physical document could be destroyed but the constitution would survive. Also, it can be changed, not by a physical change in the document, but by its reinterpretation (a change of meaning) through the court system of the country.

Consider another example of how meaning can change reality: the wedding ring. At a wedding, one partner offers the other a ring with the words, "Accept this ring as a sign of my love and fidelity." In this action, this particular ring acquires a new meaning. It is no longer just a band of gold, but it functions as a sign of something else. It has the new meaning of being a sign, which it did not have before the ceremony. This sign value is particular to this ring. To lose the ring by accident would be a great loss. Or alternatively, if the marriage broke down the ring might be removed in anger. The wedding band of a parent or grandparent might be handed down to the child or grandchild as having special significance. The reality of the ring has changed. Not every ring, but this one ring is a sign of this one love between these two people. Other people might not recognize it, but that does not change the fact that this ring has new meaning. Nor does the changed reality of this ring create any change that could be identified by any scientific investigation. Strip away the human context of meaning, of love exchanged, of lives brought together in a common bond, and it is just a gold band.

Of course, the issue here is the reality of that human world of meaning. It is not the reality investigated by physics or chemistry or biology. It is the reality of institutions, of ideologies, of legal and political systems. Even a hard-headed scientist may still wear a wedding ring as a sign of love for another; her feelings may be roused by the raising of a national flag (not just a colored piece of cloth) and the singing of the national anthem (not just air molecules vibrating); she recognizes the force of a legal contract (not just black marks on white paper) with a book publisher or for a research grant. All these things are real, not illusion.

If this human world constituted by meaning and value is in fact a real world—if its reality does not depend on its being a mere reflection of a reflection of a reflection of some "deeper" subatomic reality, but something whose reality can be intelligently grasped and reasonably affirmed independently of any knowledge of biology or biochemistry or quantum mechanics—then how much more real are the insights, judgments, and decisions that create this world. In fact, as the "creating reality," they are more important and more real than what they create. The human world of meaning and value is a reflection of the world of the human spirit. Of course, it is also true that in many ways this world "creates" us, as we are born into a preexisting world of meanings and values that shape the ways we think and feel about everything. But when we look back into history we can uncover many of the human acts, the determination of founding fathers and mothers, that established many of the features we now take for granted.

The purpose here is to make us reconceive the ways in which we think about the relative priorities of spirit and matter. To a materialist worldview, the emergence of intelligence is a random happenstance, a relative latecomer in the evolutionary process whose reality is simply epiphenomenal to underlying neural events. But once we acknowledge the real as the objective of intelligent inquiry and reasonable affirmation, we begin to invert this stance. The world of spirit starts to become more "real" inasmuch as it is creative of new realities in an unprecedented manner.

An Ambiguous Reality

Of course, this human world is not without its ambiguities. Just as the emergence of consciousness brings with it the ambiguity of pain, so too the emergence of intelligence and reason bring with them certain moral ambiguities. Just as our human world of meaning and value is created by intelligence, so too there are signs of stupidity. Just as it is governed by reason, so too there are signs of irrationality and mendacity. Intelligence and reason can be truncated by special interests, by personal bias, by short-term gain with long-term undesirable consequences, by ideologies that distort the truth about human beings, judging people by the color of their skin or their sexual identity or orientation. While the cumulative product of intelligence and reason is progress and development, the cumulative product of stupidity and unreason is decline and social dissolution.

The emergence of spirit, then, is also the beginning of the problem of evil, properly so called. Whereas pain arises from the emergence of consciousness per se, evil belongs to the realm of spirit, to the ways in which human meanings and values are implemented in decisions. This is not the place to deal directly with the problem of evil, which I consider in detail in chapter 7. Before that we still need to consider issues of values, the good, and teleology. However, it is important to recognize at this stage that the world of spirit is not unambiguous. Perhaps this is one reason people seek to escape from the human world of meaning and value into the more "real" world of the already-out-there-now reality of extroverted consciousness. In the human world, we encounter lies and falsehood, whereas in the world of the already-out-there-now real there is just data, which never lies.

God as Pure Spirit

I noted above the claim that human intelligence has the quality of being "spiritual"—that is, it enjoys a relative independence from its material basis. It can grasp infinite possibilities in a single act, not through an infinite series of discrete acts, but *in toto* in one flash. Nonetheless, this is not complete independence. As Aristotle noted and Aquinas reaffirmed, in this life intellect requires images, what they called phantasm, in order to operate correctly. Insight arises from image, taken in the generic sense of a product of imagination, be it visual, auditory, tactile, and so on. Still, the insight is more than the image. As Aristotle also noted in the comments referred to above, while strong sensory input overwhelms the senses to the point where they shut down, strong insight stimulates the intellect to greater activity. Insight adds intelligibility to the data, or meaning to the experience. But the dependence on the image always remains.

This dependence is most evident in the experience of taking a drug like alcohol. The drug affects the underlying biochemistry and hence neural functioning, so that imagination is distorted. The resulting distortion of the imagination means that intelligence no longer operates effectively; we become stupid. Similarly, in the half-awake, half-asleep state of twilight consciousness during the night, all sorts of insights occur that prove unreliable in the light of day.

Still, if the reality of intelligence and reason is more real than the human world of meaning and values that it creates—if the world of spirit has some priority over the world of matter in its power of creativity; if spirit becomes our paradigm of what is real rather than mere materiality—then should we not consider the possibility of intelligence and reason that enjoys complete independence from materiality, that does not create out of preexisting conditions but *ex nihilo*? Again, we should be reminded of Lonergan's comment that one cannot prove the existence of God to a materialist without first moving that person from their materialism. To a materialist, talk of an existence that is purely immaterial, or pure spirit, is mere fantasy. Reality is about what we can see, hear, touch, taste, and smell. Yet such a limited conception of reality can barely acknowledge the reality of the human world of meaning and value, of national constitutions and penal codes, of mortgages and interest rates, let alone the reality of the inner world of insight, judgment, and decision that produces this world of meaning and value. Why should we allow ourselves to be constrained within such a limited materialist view of what is real?

As the act of spirit is specified in terms of acts of understanding, we shall consider the possibility of a pure spirit who understands everything about everything. What could we say about such an existing reality that is pure spirit? We can raise this question as a type of metaphysical hypothesis, something that we can explore the properties of, much as physics explored the properties of the Higgs boson for decades before its existence could be determined. Whether such a being exists is a further question requiring sufficient reason to draw such a conclusion. But at least the very exploration helps us dispel mistaken and mythic notions of God's existence, which often operate in debates of this sort.

The first observation is that such an existence is strictly unimaginable. Our imaginations operate within the bounds of space and time, though we can construct symbolic systems that serve as a proxy for images from which we can still abstract intelligibility. This is particularly the case in mathematics. However, the world of pure spirit is not so imaginable, though it is not therefore beyond our experience, as the above examples of insight demonstrate. We can use proxy images for such experiences, such as "like a light going on in my head" or "the penny dropped" for insight.[14] We know there is no physical light involved, but it has something like the power of light to illuminate the objects of our knowing. However, we need to take extra care in the deployment of such images, because attending to such inner experiences requires sensitivity and practice. We readily fall into the myth of taking an "inner look" to seek out some "already-in-there-now" real "me," which we shall never find.

The second observation is that such existence is timeless or eternal. One of the clear outcomes of modern science is the inseparability of space, time, and matter. While Isaac Newton imagined a world of

14. In fact, Aquinas talks of the "light of intellect," well aware that it is not physical light, but the illumination of intelligence doing its work in seeking understanding.

separable space and time, Albert Einstein's theory of special relativity has forced us to recognize the interrelationship between the two, so that now physicists speak of space-time. Space and time are relative to motion, so that there is no single definitive time frame by which all other times can be consistently related. There is no universal notion of simultaneity. Space and time are related to motion, so that from the point of view of a "stationary" observer, time on a moving object seems to slow down. Einstein's theory of general relativity adds matter to the mix to demonstrate the interrelationship between matter (gravity), space, and time. Quantum mechanics then reveals that even empty space-time is a boiling cauldron of virtual particles and antiparticles. Time is inseparable from space and matter. As Paul Davies notes, "Time is part of the physical universe, inseparable from space and matter. Any designer/creator of the universe must therefore transcend time, as well as space and matter. That is, God must lie *outside* time if God is to be the designer and creator *of* time."[15] A being of pure spirit, which is completely independent of space and matter, is independent of time; that is, it is eternal.

Normally, we might think of eternity as the unending duration of time, a time with perhaps a beginning but with no end. But this is not what is meant by the eternity associated with pure spirit. It is not the eternity of duration but of timelessness. We have no direct understanding of what such a form of existence may be. However, we might extrapolate from our own experience of insights. Above, we began with a single insight into one specific example, but moved toward one that encompassed an infinite number of cases, all in a single insight. Can we extrapolate toward an insight that grasps not just this or that instance, but all possible intelligible realities at once?

---

15. Paul Davies, *The Goldilocks Enigma: Why Is the Universe Just Right for Life?* (London: Allen Lane, 2006), 227. For a fuller argument, see Neil Ormerod and Cynthia S. W. Crysdale, *Creator God, Evolving World* (Minneapolis: Fortress Press, 2013), 48–54.

In a single act, such a spirit would understand everything about everything. There is no change, no time, in such an act, since it is a complete act to which nothing can be added or subtracted.

Third, the existence of such a pure spirit that understands everything about everything is self-explanatory in the deepest sense. To understand everything about everything is to understand oneself as existent and to understand the very nature of one's own existence. As such, this spirit can explain its own existence; it is "self" explanatory. There is no need or possibility of any further explanation because in a single act it understands everything about everything. Whereas for us existence is a brute fact that we can verify through evidence but not explain through insight, to understand everything about everything is also to understand all existence itself.

Fourth, we can relate this to the discussion of contingent and necessary being from the previous chapter. There, I argued that scientific method has built into it a recognition of the contingency of existence. The necessity of empirical verification implies that things could be other than they are, that their existence is not self-explanatory. The existence of contingent reality remains unintelligible unless it is causally dependent on a necessary being, something whose existence is self-explanatory. A hypothetical pure spirit who understands everything about everything is self-explanatory because it can explain its own existence without reference to anything beyond itself. It would be a necessary being in that sense. Also, it would be able to explain the existence of all contingent being, because it understands everything about everything. Is the existence of contingent being then dependent upon this necessary being, this self-explanatory spirit who grasps everything about everything?

Here we need to invert our usual understanding of knowledge as in some sense receptive and focus on intelligence and reason as creative, as we have seen in the case of human intelligence and reason in relation to the world of meaning and value. In that sense, a pure spirit who grasps everything about everything does not know contingent being because it receives that knowledge from something apart from itself. Rather, its knowledge creates contingent being: *its knowledge is determinative of reality; reality is not determinative of its knowing.* Otherwise, its knowing of contingent reality would be another contingent fact requiring further explanation. This pure spirit would not then understand everything about everything.

To summarize, a pure spirit that understands everything about everything is eternal and unchanging. It is immaterial, and so grasps everything about everything in a single act of understanding. As Aquinas would say, it is pure act, *actus pura*. It is necessary being because it requires no explanation beyond itself for its own existence; it is self-explanatory. All contingent being depends upon such necessary being for its existence. It is omniscient because it understands everything about everything and so knows everything, and omnipotent because its understanding of everything about everything is the cause of all contingent being. It and it alone is the creator of everything other than itself, which itself needs no creator because it is self-explanatory. No factor is needed apart from itself to explain the existence of anything, because in one act such a being understands everything about everything. Finally, pure spirit is personal, since nothing is more personal than understanding. And again as Aquinas would say, such a being "all people call God." This hypothesis of a pure spirit who grasps everything about everything is a pretty good approximation of the classical theistic account of God found in traditional sources such as Thomas Aquinas.

From Hypothesis to Verification?

The question remains how one might move from hypothesis to verification. Are there sufficient reasons to affirm the existence of a pure spirit who understands everything about everything? Here we might refer again to Lonergan's three-line syllogism on the existence of God, as noted in chapter 1:

> If the real is completely intelligible, God exists.
>
> But the real is completely intelligible.
>
> Therefore God exists.[16]

The first line links the intelligibility of reality with the existence of God. I have noted that science hits a brick wall in terms of existence. It presupposes, but does not explain, existence. As Martin Rees states it, "Theorists may, some day, be able to write down fundamental equations governing physical reality. But physics can never explain what 'breathes fire' into the equations, and actualizes them in a real cosmos."[17] Existence of material reality is a brute fact, something that calls for further explanation. In metaphysical terms, our material world is contingent, not self-explanatory. It becomes completely intelligible if there is a being whose own existence is self-explanatory, necessary, and on which contingent being depends for its existence. Such a being has the characteristics that are normally associated with the divine in the classical theistic tradition.

The second line is then the point of contention. Is the real completely intelligible? The key to this aspect of the proof lies in the event of intellectual conversion. Such a conversion involves a shift in one's criteria of reality from the already-out-there-now real of

---

16. Lonergan, *Insight*, 695.
17. Martin J. Rees, *Just Six Numbers: The Deep Forces That Shape the Universe* (New York: Basic Books, 2000), 131.

extroverted consciousness to the criteria of intelligence and reason as determinative of reality. These criteria are implicit in the scientific method; thus they are not opposed to science, but are in fact the very presupposition of all science. Intellectual conversion also allows us to escape the flawed reductionism that denies reality to all but the smallest components of particle physics, as if they are somehow more real than our world of meanings and values.

Inasmuch as we are committed to such an intellectual conversion, reality and affirmed intelligibility correlate as known and knowing. That which is unintelligible and unreasonable is a mere nothing. It is a nonexistent phantom to be discarded, like the Manichaeism that Nebridius demolished by demonstrating its unintelligibility and unreasonableness, or like the hypothesis that the square root of two is rational is to be discarded by demonstrating the absurd consequences of such a hypothesis. Implicitly and unreflectively, we reject the notion that reality is unintelligible and unreasonable. Intellectual conversion involves moving that rejection from the implicit to the explicit, from the unreflective to the reflective. Such an intellectual conversion is not just a logical deduction from more basic premises but a new horizon that determines the meaning of all basic premises about reality, being, and existence. *It emerges as a commitment and a conviction.* If it is not present, reality remains to some extent a mixture of the intelligible and the unintelligible, and proving God's existence remains elusive.

On the other hand, it is difficult if not impossible to argue against the position that reality is completely intelligible. Any argument against it must propose intelligent and reasonable contentions as to why reality does not conform to the demands of intelligence and reason. But if reality does not conform to the demands of intelligence and reason, what is the value of this argument? The presupposition of the argument is precisely that reality is completely intelligible, for unless that is the case, no intelligent and reasonable argument has any necessary traction in the real world.

Conclusion

The prior issue, then, for any natural theology is the presence or absence—and indeed the cultural prevalence—of intellectual conversion. Making such an issue explicit is the required therapeutic for reason in our present age. We have seen how such a conversion is implicit in the scientific method, and in fact in any methodology for moving from data, to hypothesis formation, to established conclusion.

But in our present age this therapeutic must deal with the persistent myth of reality as the already-out-there-now real of extroverted consciousness. This myth results in the most oppressive reductionism imaginable, stripping reality from everything except the most basic elementary particles of subatomic physics. Intellectual conversion, on the other hand, liberates intelligence and reason to be fully intelligent and reasonable by marrying our criteria for knowing (intelligence and reason) with our criteria for reality (intelligibility and reasonability). This is the true beginning of metaphysics, and within this horizon we can begin to properly address the God question. It opens up for us the reality of the inner world of intelligence and reason, or spirit, and allows us to begin to properly conceive what it might mean to affirm the existence of a pure spirit who understands everything about everything. The fragility of the conclusion of the existence of such a being, whom all people call God, is then the fragility of intellectual conversion itself.

5

Morality, Responsibility, and God

So far, I have mainly discussed intelligibility and reasonableness, intelligence and reason, and meaning and truth, but have said little about the good and issues of ethics and morality. In a sense, my primary interlocutors have been those who promote the supposed disjunction between science and religious belief, so the focus has remained on how intelligence and reason, which lie at the heart of the scientific enterprise, lead naturally to the God question through the recognition of the intelligibility and contingency of our universe. This contingency is revealed in the fact that no scientific theory is self-verifying; the movement from hypothesis to established account must accommodate the brute fact of existence, which is given or not given in the evidence, but is not explained. The notion of a necessary being emerges as an explanation for the rest of contingent being (chapter 3). In classical terms, this is to focus on the question of God's efficient causality. God is the efficient cause of being, or as Martin Rees put it, God "breathes fire" into the equations that science proposes. We explored this further by considering the notion of a pure spirit that understands everything about everything in a single act of insight (chapter 4). From this, we grasped how intellectual conversion might lead one to affirm the existence of such a pure spirit.

We must now take up the question of the good, the nature of moral obligation, and the purposefulness of creation. This can then lead us to a fuller discussion of the political dimension of natural theology, because the polis is one instance, and a very important one, of the human good. However, this is to move beyond the notion of God as efficient cause and to begin to consider God as final cause.

This does not entail ignoring the gains made in previous chapters. Indeed, to begin to think intelligently and reasonably about the nature of the good is to assume that the good is intelligible and open to reasonable discussion. This moves the discussion beyond the notion of the good as arbitrary, or purely subjective, or the product of our spontaneous desires. However, to begin to move in this direction we must unpack the implicit teleology or purposefulness of intelligence and reason.

It is important to state at the outset that the issue at stake here is not moral performance per se, but the nature of the good and of morality. Undoubtedly, there are many atheists who are fine moral persons, and many morally reprehensible people who are religious believers. That is not the issue here. The issue is our ability to give a coherent account of the nature of morality, and whether this is in some way dependent on belief in the existence of God. The relationship between moral performance and religious belief is more complex, but it really takes us beyond questions approachable through "reason" and raises strictly theological issues of sin, original sin, and grace, which are beyond the scope of this present work.[1]

---

1. See Neil Ormerod, *Creation, Grace and Redemption* (Maryknoll, NY: Orbis, 2007), for an account of these issues.

The Implicit Teleology of Richard Dawkins

The basic claim of many atheists is that science reveals the universe to be a meaningless, purposeless place. There is no God behind it all to create meaning or give some secret purpose that we must uncover or have revealed to us. We are conceived, born, live, and die like all the other animals, with no higher meaning or purpose to it all. Once we accept this fact and fate, we should settle down and make the most of it by enjoying ourselves and trying not to hurt others, avoiding pain as much as we can and then dying, again hopefully as painlessly as possible. The best advice that Richard Dawkins seems to be able to come up with is "enjoy your own sex lives" and "don't indoctrinate your children."[2] However, there is more to Dawkins's position than he himself might understand.

In the preface to his bestselling book *The God Delusion*, Dawkins provides the reader with his basic reason for writing it: "If this book works as I intend, the religious readers who open it will be atheists when they put it down."[3] While many of his followers will undoubtedly think this is a fine and noble aim, it is worthwhile to pause a while and ask ourselves what such a claim means and what it presupposes, for it is possible to draw from it a contradiction between what Dawkins proposes and his actual performance as an author.

Put directly, Dawkins's book is a prolonged argument against religious belief. It promotes a scientific worldview as contrary to religious beliefs and argues that maintaining such beliefs in the face of the dominance of this worldview is nothing less than irrational. The unbeliever is reasonable and the believer is deluded, as the title of his book suggests. If you read his book and you are a reasonable person,

2. Richard Dawkins, *The God Delusion* (London: Bantam, 2006), 264.
3. Ibid., 5.

you will come to the same conclusion as Dawkins; if you don't, either you are lacking in rationality or are dishonest (or both).

What assumptions are operating in such a stance? What implicit understanding of human beings is presumed in Dawkins's performance? The first assumption is that human beings are reasoning beings, that they can follow arguments and evidence and come to a reasonable conclusion. Indeed, the primacy of reason is central to the scientific enterprise, as he regularly reminds his readers. This much is explicit. However, there is also a second assumption, less explicit, that the dictates of reason have the power to compel human decisions and actions, that they have a normative significance for human living. Implicit in Dawkins's understanding of human beings is that if a belief *is* irrational, then one *should* not follow or uphold it. To be irrational or dishonest in the face of reason is somehow to fail in what it means to be fully and properly human.

Two points are worth noting here. First, Dawkins has implicitly moved from a matter of fact (a belief *is* irrational) to a moral conclusion (one *should* not uphold such a belief). He has moved from an "is" to an "ought." David Hume famously argued that one cannot derive an "ought" from an "is," but Alasdair MacIntyre has countered that Hume's argument fails when the reality under consideration has an end or purpose.[4] A watch has the purpose of telling the time; if it fails to do so it is not a very good watch, it is not doing what a watch ought to do. In moving from an "is" to an "ought," Dawkins is imbuing human beings with a purpose, which is to live according to the dictates of reason. To fail to do so is to attract contempt for failing to live as human beings should live, a contempt that Dawkins and his followers are more than willing to direct at religious believers.[5] This movement from an "is" to an "ought" was always the point

4. Alasdair MacIntyre, *After Virtue: A Study in Moral Theory*, 2nd ed. (Notre Dame, IN: University of Notre Dame Press, 1984), 57–59.

of the classic Aristotelian and Scholastic definition of human beings as "rational animals." It is not just that human beings *are* capable of reasoning, but that reason *should* guide our living. It is not just a statement of fact ("is"), but a normative account of human existence ("ought").

Second, this says something about Dawkins's implicit understanding of free will. With the Scholastics, he implicitly holds that will is "rational appetite"—that is, an orientation, desire, or need to do what is reasonable and not do what is unreasonable. In that case, free will is not some arbitrary power to choose this or that, with the choice being a matter of indifference; rather, it has a normative structure to it so that an act of choice can fail to do what it is meant to do. People can choose to do what is irrational, but in doing so they act against what it means to be human. Thus human beings are not just *intelligent* and *reasonable*, they are *responsible* for their decisions, which either succeed or fail to be intelligent and reasonable. As such, human beings can be held to account for their decisions and actions.

Now, it is a big claim that human actions should be based on intelligence and reason, and that we are responsible for our success or failure to do so. It is also a claim that is impossible to argue against. To argue against it would require putting forward intelligent reasons why this is not the case, and hence argue that one should not be bound by the claims of intelligence and reason. This would be a performative contradiction. One would be evoking the very structure of intelligence, reason, and responsibility that one is seeking to deny.

This same sort of performative contradiction is present in Dawkins's position. Implicitly he is appealing to intelligence, reason,

---

5. See Alister E. McGrath, *Why God Won't Go Away: Is the New Atheism Running on Empty?* (Nashville: Thomas Nelson, 2010), for an account of some of the vitriol and contempt demonstrated on new atheist websites toward believers.

and responsibility in his claim, "If this book works as I intend, the religious readers who open it will be atheists when they put it down."[6] However, his own account of morality is biologically reductionist. He explicitly denies the very purposefulness that he implicitly appeals to in writing his book.

Is Morality Biologically Derived?

Dawkins commonly argues that human morality is biologically derived. He is able to do this because he presents a truncated view of human morality that understands it as basically about altruism. In his early work *The Selfish Gene*, Dawkins argues that altruism is simply a by-product of our genetic heritage whereby our genes seek to preserve their particular genetic line.[7] There is thus a biological imperative not only to preserve my own life, but also the lives of others with whom I share a common gene pool. Altruism is therefore a biologically driven orientation, something that provides species with an evolutionary advantage because it ensures the survival of the species through the sacrifice of individual wants and needs for the sake of the whole.

Fascinating and even as plausible as this may seem, it has no bearing on Dawkins's own implicit appeal to reason as the basis for changing one's behavior. Once again, we are faced with the question of whether intelligence and reason are reducible to biology. Just as it is difficult to understand what, if any, the biological or evolutionary advantage is in being able to prove Fermat's Last Theorem, so too it is difficult to understand how the *purposefulness* of rationality—its inner exigency toward intelligence, reason, and responsibility—can

6. Dawkins, *The God Delusion*, 5.
7. Richard Dawkins, *The Selfish Gene*, 30th anniversary ed. (Oxford/New York: Oxford University Press, 2006).

be derived from a *purposeless* biological evolution. Biological evolution might explain why we *do* do something, but it cannot explain why we *should* do something. Yet implicitly, Dawkins is arguing that we *should* change our minds on the God question because of the arguments he presents in *The God Delusion*. If, in fact, his position on the biological origins of apparent morality is correct, then what are we to make of Dawkins's own performance in his book? If arguing, including Dawkins's own arguing, may be reduced to a biological function rather than a search for truth and goodness, then Nietzsche is right and all truth claims are simply an exercise of the "will to power," the desire to assert dominance over the other.

Indeed, the claim that morality can be reduced to biology is inherently implausible and trivializing. Consider one of the great moral dilemmas of our present day, whose force was recognized by Socrates and Plato over two thousand years ago: is it better to suffer evil rather than do evil? In the words of political philosopher Eric Voegelin, Socrates is debating Callicles on this very question in Plato's dialogue *Gorgias*:

> The existential issue between Socrates and Callicles can now be taken up in earnest. Socrates restates the order of evils: (1) it is bad to suffer injustice; (2) it is worse to commit injustice; (3) it is worst to remain in the dis-order of the soul which is created by doing injustice and not to experience the restoration of this order through punishment. . . . Callicles had taken the stand that it was of supreme importance to protect oneself effectively against suffering injustice. Socrates maintains that the price of safety against injustice may be too high.[8]

In the present context, the issue continues to arise around questions of torture and indefinite detention in places like Guantanamo Bay.

8. Eric Voegelin, "The Philosophy of Existence: Plato's 'Gorgias,'" *The Review of Politics* 11/4 (1949): 477–98, at 490. With some sense of providence, I first read this article in 2009 while the Obama administration was debating with Donald Rumsfeld over the morality of Guantanamo Bay. The parallels were striking.

To suffer injustice from terrorist attacks is something that we would prefer to avoid. But should we be willing to act unjustly ourselves in order to avoid the injustice of terrorism? Can we detain people without due legal process and torture them in the hope that this will enable us to prevent some future terrorist attack? This is the type of question that Socrates took with utmost seriousness, to the point where he willingly submitted to execution rather than flee his jailers. He preferred to suffer the evil of an unjust verdict rather than violate his own integrity by flight. The exigency to live intelligently, reasonably, and responsibly, to be a person of moral integrity, can come at a high price. But as Jesus once commented, better to lose the world and save one's soul than to gain the world and lose one's soul (Matthew 16:25-26). Socrates and Plato would have agreed. What possible biological advantage is it to die for the sake of one's own moral integrity? Indeed, if anything we tend to honor people who put their lives and well-being at risk on matters of moral principle—for example, Thomas More, Mohandas Gandhi, and Nelson Mandela. These people reveal to us that some things are more important than the maintenance of biological life.

This highlights a further important distinction between morality and the biological order. Biologically, there are clear immanent sanctions to being a failed member of one's species. Genetic failures may be spontaneously aborted while the less successful may fall prey to the hunter because of lack of speed, or as a hunter they may fail to gain food and so starve. The weak are culled out; the stronger, faster members live to give their genetic inheritance to the next generation. But what are the sanctions for failing to live intelligently, reasonably, and responsibly? Adhering to these imperatives might in fact be biologically disadvantageous. Ignoring them completely might yield a rich harvest of offspring. Genghis Khan and his sons raped and pillaged their way across Asia and Eastern Europe to such an extent that some 8 percent of the Asian population is thought to have descended from him.[9] Yet we do not hold him up as an example of moral flourishing. There may be some social sanctions for those who fail as moral human beings—like ostracism or ridicule—but often such people can hide their errors and even benefit from them to gain social acceptability. Thus robber barons turn into philanthropists to assuage their consciences.

Still, there are sanctions in the moral life that operate more subtly, like a growing disjunction between the person and the real world of relationships, friendships, community, and purpose. Lives can fall into cycles of violence and addiction, of repeated dishonesty and the breakdown of trust with one's former friends. Such outcomes, however, have a statistical nature to them (in the same sense that smoking causes cancer with a certain statistical likelihood), so that even three thousand years ago the psalmist could note that the evil prosper while the good struggle. This raises the crucial question, To whom are we responsible? Clearly, there is a sense in which we are responsible to one another, and we have a responsibility to ourselves to behave according to the dictates of reason. But if we flout these responsibilities and escape many of the sanctions the moral life would seek to impose upon us, so what?

Nonetheless, the exigency of living according to the norms of intelligence, reason, and responsibility remains. We cannot escape it, for it defines what it means to be human. All this is implicit in Dawkins's desire, "If this book works as I intend, the religious readers who open it will be atheists when they put it down."[10]

---

9. Tatiana Zerjal et al., "The Genetic Legacy of the Mongols," *American Journal of Human Genetics* 72/3 (2003): 717–21.

10. Dawkins, *The God Delusion*, 5.

A Metaphysics of the Good

Human decisions then are oriented to reason. A bad decision is one that has bad reasons, or can be shown to be irrational. And so Nebridius's argument against the Manichaeans left Augustine and his friends puzzled. They could feel the force of the argument and where it was pushing them, though at the time they were still unwilling to move. A good decision is one for which there are good reasons, sufficient to justify undertaking the task. In metaphysical terms, this is what Augustine would mean later in Book 7 of *The Confessions* when he would develop his metaphysics of evil, of evil as having no substance. There is a lack of substantial reasons for an evil action to occur. Good decisions add to the (well-)being of the world, while bad decisions detract from it.

Nonetheless, while it is sometimes possible to point to an incoherence or irrationality in a person's actions, it is often less clear what constitutes a good reason to do something. Hence we have no difficulty chastising someone whose beliefs are irrational, but it is not as easy to identify what beliefs might be considered rational. It is easier to identify examples of non-flourishing than it is to specify what it would mean for something to flourish. In general, however, when people seek to justify their actions they will refer to values and disvalues of some sort. I act this way because I seek to achieve this value, or seek to avoid this disvalue. So we can relate the question of human flourishing to that of values.

Values, however, are a puzzling notion. Suppose we ask why someone acts in a particular way. They respond, "Because I value X." This is meant to provide a reason for the action. Still one can ask, "Why do you value X?" Valuing is itself a decision or stance, but what justifies this as a good decision or stance? If I seek to push it back to some more primitive value (Y), I could end up in an infinite regress, so I may as well simply assert that X is good and be done with it. One way to deal with this givenness is to say that all people have their own value system, their choice of said system is basically arbitrary, and values are irreducibly subjective and pluralistic. Then there is no objective morality or account of human flourishing, and all are free to go their own way. In fact, much of Western liberal culture seems to operate on this premise. All people are entitled to their own values, as long as they do not impinge upon or harm others.

Alternatively, we could say that it is not that values are good because we value them, but we value them because they are in fact valuable in some objective or given sense.[11] Then our freedom consists in our freely conforming ourselves to a set of values that is not of our making, but that are constitutive of what it means to be a flourishing human being. Further, we must then learn to value what is truly of value; it is not automatic or spontaneous, but something we are educated into.[12] Often, this learning will be through a concrete experience of the value in question, through repeated exposure or some other form of moral formation.[13] Without such an education, we can be blind to the real value present in an experience or event. In the end, we have no choice about the values that constitute human flourishing; they are given in the very structure of being human.

11. This is a more anthropocentric version of Euthyphro's dilemma, "Is the pious loved by the gods because it is pious, or is it pious because it is loved by the gods?" found in Plato's dialogue *Euthyphro*.

12. The myth of spontaneous desire has been thoroughly deconstructed by René Girard's notion of mimetic desire. We learn to desire through the desires of others, not through some spontaneous desire that somehow defines my identity. See René Girard, Jean-Michel Oughourlian, and Guy Lefort, *Things Hidden since the Foundation of the World* (Stanford, CA: Stanford University Press, 1987).

13. Dawkins would probably dismiss such a claim as seeking to justify "indoctrination." However, no parents raise their children in a "value-free" environment and then hope the children will discover or decide what is of value on their own when they are adults. On reaching adulthood, such children are unlikely to be able to hit on good values on their own and will either reproduce the value system of their parents as best they can or easily fall into the various forms of self-indulgence promoted in a hyper-consumerist society.

This is exactly what we found in Dawkins's implicit appeal to the power of reason to shape our decisions and beliefs. The demand to reject irrational beliefs is not something of our own choosing. Irrationality *is* a disvalue for human beings. We cannot "freely" take it up or put it aside, as if it is an arbitrary choice on our part. It defines what it means to be human, to be a "rational animal." We have no choice about it. To fail to recognize this value is to fail in something essential to being human.

One might conclude that values are irreducible or basic (not derived from something more primitive), yet normative. They are given in some sense objectively, that is, independent of our choosing. Further, as real, they are still intelligible in their givenness. Just as the chemist takes the chemical elements as a given and then sets out to understand their interrelatedness, resulting in the periodic table, so in seeking to understand values we can take them as given and seek to understand them in their interrelatedness.

And just as a chemist must uncover the full range of chemical elements empirically, so too we must uncover the full range of human values empirically. We learn what is of value in life by living life, not through some a priori deduction. The value of the scientific method, for example, is not obvious to a child or to most nonscientists. Nonetheless, we can learn its value through its use and come to appreciate its power in understanding reality. Similarly, the value of art, of poetry, of great literature all take time and effort to appreciate, but having done so they repay us a thousandfold. Moral education, the learning and acquisition of values and the recognition of disvalues, is inevitably a tradition-based process that involves learning and reasoning about what has been learned to be of value through past experiments in human flourishing.[14] This is not to place such

---

14. This is brought out most clearly in the work of Alasdair MacIntyre, particularly *Whose Justice? Which Rationality?* (Notre Dame, IN: University of Notre Dame Press, 1988).

traditions beyond question. When two distinct cultures begin to interact, there can be much mutual learning as two bodies of meaning and value come into contact and dialogue.

With these provisos in place, I will now seek to deploy a hierarchical scale of values. As *hierarchical*, it seeks to place different types of values into relationship with one another, thus arguing for an intelligible structure among the full range of values. As a scale of *values*, it does not arise from some a priori deduction but from reflecting on the goodness of human living. It is not original to me but arises in the writings of Bernard Lonergan.[15] It stands or falls on whether it gives an adequate account of the values we use to justify our actions and the relative weighting we give those values.

Even so, its plausibility requires some personal familiarity with the values in question. Here there arises a question not just of intellectual conversion but of moral conversion, whereby we move from mere satisfactions and dissatisfactions (seeking pleasure and avoiding pain)[16] to what are truly valuable as our criteria for decisions. Just as a metaphysics of the real requires some form of intellectual conversion, so a metaphysics of the good requires some form of moral conversion.

A Scale of Values

We begin with *vital* values, the goods of health and vitality, of strength and physical graciousness, of reproduction and biological generativity. These values have a strongly biological basis, and we are increasingly aware that maintaining them is a question not just of individual responsibility but of our larger-scale care for the earth and

15. Bernard J. F. Lonergan, *Method in Theology* (London: DLT, 1972).
16. Such criteria lead to the pseudo-rationality of a "calculus of pleasure and pain" and the maximizing of pleasure and the minimizing of pain for the greatest number of people as criteria for personal and social decision-making. These are the criteria of a moral child, not of a morally converted adult.

its attendant biosphere. Biological life is the starting point for human values, and this life is dependent on the well-being of the whole ecosphere for its continuance. Still, these vital values must be placed into relationship with the inevitability of loss, of illness and eventual death. The biological cycle of birth, life, and death is a constant for human existence. No amount of seeking to maintain vital values will allow us to escape the inevitability of aging and death. Every reasonable person knows this.

While vital values are the beginning of human values, the recurrent meeting of those values is not to be found in individual effort but through the cooperative coordination of the production and distribution of goods, which forms *social* values. Here the spontaneous identification of social groups (with undoubtedly a strong biological foundation) is transformed into a social polity of family, tribe, kingdom, and nation, with an emerging technology that forms the material basis for an increasingly coordinated economy of the production and distribution of goods and services. These then maintain our vitality while adding a new level of the good: the good of order. This good requires that we not just eat, mate, sleep, and die, but that we be good citizens who contribute to the common good, to technological development, to economic production and distribution, and to political process. Commonly, we recognize that these values are higher than the vital values of individual members of the polity. If the good of the social order is seriously threatened by marauding hordes of foreign invaders, a nation may call upon its citizens to defend the good of social order, even at the cost of loss of life. To fail to answer such a call might be thought of as cowardice.[17]

Social values give rise to further questions. Once the vital values of most of the citizenry are being met, there may be the leisure to ask

---

17. This is not to deny the possibility of conscientious objection to military service, but such objection arises from an even higher level of value, that of personal value.

questions about the form of social ordering: Which is the best form of polity or social ordering? What goods should our economy produce? What leads to human flourishing itself? What is the meaning and purpose of life? These questions may be addressed in a variety of forms: in art, literature, and drama, or in more didactic forms in philosophy and theology. Thus a good social order leads to the emergence of *cultural* values, where the meaning and purpose of living, of the best form of political ordering, of the purpose of intellectual pursuits such as science, philosophy, history and theology can be hammered out for each successive generation. Indeed, I have already appealed to a structure for cultural values in chapter 2, where I spoke of cosmological and anthropological cultural types. Cultural values require a more refined moral sensibility for their appreciation than do vital and social values. Not everyone will appreciate the value of great literature or the philosophical classics. Nonetheless, these have the power to shape civilizations over centuries, and so are more important or higher than either vital or social values.

Cultural values shape the moral imaginations of a society. We are all born into a preexisting social and cultural context; through our education and life experience we are taught to value aspects of our context, to display an appropriate level of patriotism, to aspire to the cultural achievements of our society, and so on. Still, the time will arise when we must come to our own decisions regarding our context, to affirm its values and to criticize its disvalues. And so emerges the question of *personal* values. Can I transcend the values of my context? Can I critique the liberal consumer society that I grew up in? Or a society that promotes racial division? Can I conscientiously object to a war, even though it might mean imprisonment and perhaps even death, because I judge the war unjust? Is it better to suffer injustice than to act unjustly? What price my moral integrity? These are the existential questions every moral agent must face as a human being. Do I just go with the flow of my social and cultural context, or can I take a critical stance, even though it may cost me dearly? To appreciate the depth of such questions is to grasp what is meant by personal values.

The question may finally arise whether this is the highest level of value that we can appreciate. Is there a higher court of appeal than the personal, a value that "trumps" all others in the moral life? And if so, what is its relationship to the other values we have considered? This again raises the question of God. If belief in God is reasonable, precisely as the necessary cause of all that is, then God is the source of all value. And we have the values we have because this is how we have been made. As the source of all goodness, God too is good, indeed the highest good. Any good that exists owes its existence to God; any good that might come to exist comes to exist because God creates it, gives it being. If acting according to the dictates of intelligence and reason is the basis of being responsible, of moral goodness, then God, who understands everything about everything, whose very existence relegates the unintelligible and unreasonable to a state of nonexistence, is fully committed to the intelligence and reasonableness of decision. Divine action is fully in accord with divine intelligence and reason, and so God is fully and unalterably good.

To Whom Are We Responsible?

I noted above the question of the sanctions that flow from the moral demand to be intelligent, reasonable, and responsible. These sanctions are not like the sanctions of the biological order, which are built into the evolutionary process of natural selection. There are some similarities in that both sets of sanctions are effective in a statistical sense, so that both the weak and the immoral may survive and even flourish at times. However, a well-ordered society seeks to minimize the ability of the wicked to flourish by adding legal sanctions to the most egregious forms of socially immoral behaviors such as theft or murder. But even so, history is littered with murderers, particularly those who have used political power to eliminate a vast number of people—Hitler in Germany, Pol Pot in Cambodia, Joseph Stalin in the Soviet Union, and so on—and who seem to escape any form of social sanction whatsoever during their lifetime. Perhaps their families might carry social opprobrium, but they themselves die without any hope of earthly justice redressing their crimes.

Human efforts to develop and apply sanctions to such egregious human immorality are at best hit-and-miss and at worse seem to exacerbate the problem, making prisons into schools for criminal education. Yet these efforts recognize the need to call us to account for our decisions, to make us accountable for our actions, particularly when they impact other people in a significant way. There is an exigency toward intelligence, reason, and responsibility that demands some form of accountability, yet such accountability cannot be achieved through merely human means. Indeed, attempts to produce accountability through political processes alone often seem to produce little more than "hell on earth."[18]

What does atheism have to offer in such a situation? Little more than platitudes. In the end, without the existence of God as one to whom we are accountable for our actions, our inner exigency to be responsible can find no one to whom we are ultimately responsible and identify no final sanctions against being irresponsible. We may recall Socrates's debate with Callicles, noted above. Socrates argued that while it is not good to suffer evil, it is worse to do evil in seeking

---

18. See Anthony Kelly, *Eschatology and Hope*, Theology in Global Perspective (Maryknoll, NY: Orbis, 2006), 138–41.

to avoid that evil. Still, "It is worst to remain in the dis-order of the soul which is created by doing injustice and not to experience the restoration of this order through punishment."[19] The right order of the soul needs to be restored, and to remain in such disorder is the greatest evil. It is not pleasant to recognize one's failure to act according to the dictates of intelligence, reason, and responsibility; one must renounce one's own actions and seek to undo the harm one has done. One must take responsibility for one's irresponsible actions.

Here it is worth recalling Kant's requirement for holding to the immortality of the soul and the existence of God as demands of practical reason. While Kant held that neither of these positions is provable by pure reason, his stance on this is conditioned by his holding to the noumena-phenomena distinction, which does not stand once intellectual conversion has taken place. Kant recognized that without these two precepts of practical reason, the moral life was void of any ultimate meaning.[20] In the previous chapter, we noted the types of reasons one might put forward for both the separability of the intellect (the natural immortality of the soul) and for the existence of God as a pure spirit who understands everything about everything. With these two precepts within the grasp of reason, we can affirm the meaningfulness of the moral life, not just for this life, but also for life beyond the grave.

This is not to posit some extrinsic system of rewards and punishments as motivation for the moral life, though it may act as such for those who have a loose grip on the nature of their own exigency toward intelligence, reasonableness, and responsibility. The rewards and punishments may be no more than to be eternally what my actions have made me to be: either eternally and fully committed

---

19. Voegelin, "The Philosophy of Existence: Plato's 'Gorgias,'" 490.
20. Kant also included the existence of freedom, which I have already argued for above in terms of the exigency to be responsible.

to the life of intelligence, reasonableness, and responsibility, or eternally locked into stupidity, silliness, and irresponsibility.[21]

However, the existence of God also means that human failing is not the final word. Precisely because God exists as the one to whom we are accountable, there is also the possibility of forgiveness, offered not just in the light of repentance but as a gift that promotes repentance and personal transformation. As the source of all goodness, God takes no delight in seeing human beings locked into stupidity, silliness, and irresponsibility. Such a stance is the antithesis of God's own being. Forgiveness is one way of resolving such an antithesis, but it cannot mean an evasion of responsibility, as if nothing matters in the long run. It must involve the full acceptance of one's responsibility for being so stupid, silly, and irresponsible. This acceptance is not pleasant in this life, nor is it likely to be pleasant in the next; but the question of how and in what ways it might occur is beyond our immediate concern here, and best left to God. On the other hand, some form of union with God would be a union with the source of all meaning, truth, and goodness, and so constitute the fulfillment of all our longings for these elusive goals. We would then know as fully as we are known.

God's Freedom versus Human Freedom

While some would seek to eliminate God by referring to the findings of modern science, others would seek to eliminate God in the name of human freedom. If God is the cause of all contingent existence, then God is also the cause of my own actions; God's timelessness means that for God the future is as thoroughly known as the past, so that while I might think of my acts as free, really they are nothing

---

21. For a classic parable of what such an existence might be like, see C. S. Lewis, *The Great Divorce* (New York: HarperCollins, 2001).

more than the outworking of a divine creation over which I really have no control. My freedom would then be an illusion. However, with the reality of human freedom, it is the existence of God that proves illusory. Either God's freedom is determinative of our actions, or human freedom is. The two cannot coexist.[22]

Now in the present work, I have upheld that God is the cause of all contingent existence, and also that human freedom is the condition for the possibility of a reasoned argument changing anyone's beliefs. How can we avoid the apparent contradiction between these two as presented by the argument in the previous paragraph? Here I would draw on a Scholastic distinction between primary and secondary causation. This is implicit in Martin Rees's distinction between the ability to write down the equations that govern physical laws and what "breathes fire" into the equations.[23] As the cause of all contingent being, God is the one who breathes fire into the equations; in Scholastic terms, God is the primary cause of being. But this does not deny the real but secondary causation of scientific explanations for how and why things do what they do. Gravity really causes things to fall, according to laws explicated by Newton and Einstein. Smoking really causes lung cancer, though through a form of statistical causation. And I am the real cause of my own decisions, freely undertaken.[24] But the existence of gravity, of cigarettes and lung cancer, and of my human freedom are not self-explanatory. Each depends on something else in order to be, and ultimately on

22. This argument is often attributed to Jean-Paul Sartre. He is at times quoted as saying, "If God exists then the future is determined and I am not free. I am free; therefore God does not exist," with the source given as *Being and Nothingness*, part 4, ch. 1. There is no such exact quote in *Being and Nothingness*, though it is a succinct summary of Sartre's argument. My thanks to Elizabeth Murray for confirming this.
23. Martin J. Rees, *Just Six Numbers: The Deep Forces that Shape the Universe* (New York: Basic Books, 2000), 131.
24. For a fuller account of classical and statistical forms of causation, see Neil Ormerod and Cynthia S. W. Crysdale, *Creator God, Evolving World* (Minneapolis: Fortress Press, 2013).

God as the self-explanatory cause of all existence. If God causes human beings to be free, to truly exercise a genuine freedom for which they are responsible and accountable, then that is how human beings truly are.

This distinction between primary and secondary causation corresponds to what Kathryn Tanner captures in her notion that the relationship between God and the creature is noncompetitive.[25] Human and divine freedom do not compete with one another because they operate at different explanatory levels. The argument that pits God's existence and human freedom against one another then loses its force. The future is known by God, but it is known precisely as the product of genuine secondary causes that bring it about, including the secondary causes of free human actions, which, if God did not cause them to be and did not know them to exist, would not be at all. But because God does cause them to be, and does know them into existence, they are what they truly are: genuine secondary causes. God freely makes me to be free.

However, we must also ask whether we might enter into a personal relationship with God and what this might mean. Can we draw closer to God through conforming ourselves more closely to the source of all meaning, truth, and goodness? Would this not make me more free rather than less free? Can we learn an ever-greater appreciation of God as good, as the highest good, who is then the goal of all my striving for meaning, truth, and goodness? And may God, too, play an active role in reaching out to our human condition, seeking to empower people whose lives are no longer in their control, who need to hand themselves over to a "higher power," as practiced in various 12-step programs? Here we move beyond the bounds of natural theology per se and into questions of what constitutes a religious

---

25. Kathryn Tanner, *God and Creation in Christian Theology: Tyranny and Empowerment?* (Minneapolis: Fortress Press, 2004), 36–48, 62–64.

life, of the human search for meaning, truth, and goodness, and the possibility of a divine initiative entering into human history and transforming us from within. To address this issue, we would need to consider religions as manifest in human history and their claims to revealing a human orientation to the divine and responsiveness to divine initiative. That would be beyond the scope of the present project. However, we shall return to some of these issues in chapter 7 on theodicy.

Conclusion

This chapter began with a consideration of the implicit teleology of Richard Dawkins's claim, "If this book works as I intend, the religious readers who open it will be atheists when they put it down."[26] As opposed to the explicit aim of Dawkins's book, that implicit teleology has led us to examine human freedom and its orientation to intelligibility, reasonableness, and responsibility, or meaning, truth, and goodness, and to eventually address again the question of God as the source of all meaning, truth, and goodness, together with its implication for human existence. While I happily acknowledge the fact that those without explicit religious beliefs may lead moral lives, it is another question altogether whether they can give a coherent account of what constitutes the moral life without reference to God. Certainly, the implicit teleology of Dawkins's stance orients us more toward God than away from God.

In the next chapter, we turn our attention to one particular aspect of the good: the political order of society. In our present context, the relationship between belief in God and the political significance of that belief cannot be ignored. While in the present chapter I was

26. Dawkins, *The God Delusion*, 5.

reluctant to examine how religious traditions relate to the question of what the religious life might mean and how it might be lived, in the next chapter I take the existence of religious traditions as a historical given and ask how they might relate to the life of the political communities to which they belong.

6

———

God and Politics

One of the inescapable aspects of the debate initiated by the new atheism is the place of religion in the public square. Much of the heat, if not light, generated by the debate is caused by the background of 9/11 and the specter of Islamic radicalism seeking to establish sharia law and Islamic theocratic states around the world. This is particularly evident in the title of Christopher Hitchens's book *God Is Not Great: How Religion Poisons Everything*, with its none-too-subtle reference to a basic Islamic statement of faith, "God is great."[1] Christianity, too, contains elements that would be happy to dominate the public square. Some within Christianity look back to the era of Christendom as an ideal to be reestablished in the future, where Christianity will once again enjoy the privilege, protection, and social authority it did in the distant past.[2]

---

1. Christopher Hitchens, *God Is Not Great: How Religion Poisons Everything*, 1st ed. (New York: Twelve, 2007). Indeed, Hitchens mentions 9/11 seven times during his book.
2. One might note, as examples of this romanticism, institutions such as Christendom College, which place a heavy emphasis on the work of Thomas Aquinas and a relative lack of offerings in science, which has fundamentally shaped the modern world and our understanding of it.

Why should a natural theology in particular concern itself with the issue of the relationship between God and politics? If a natural theology succeeds in asking and to some extent answering the God question in the public arena without appeal to any particular religious tradition, then the public marginalization of God begins to look suspect. If reason in fact leads us to God in a limited but nonetheless real way, then the issue of God can and must be addressed in the public and hence political realm. However, all too often in debates about the place of God in politics, the only alternatives that we seem to be able to imagine are either complete secularization of the public and political realm or the complete dominance of that realm by a religious agenda. A natural theology that fails to address this issue fails to address one of the basic anxieties about the public raising of the God question in the present context.

Many take the supposed "separation" of church and state as itself holy writ, failing to recognize the very circumstances that led to this separation and their historical contingency. So any attempt to address the issue needs to begin with a broader analysis of the ways in which church-state or God-politics issues have been dealt with in the past, how we arrived at the present situation, and how we might move beyond this situation into a different resolution of the problems the present situation was meant to resolve.

In addressing this issue, I am very aware of the Christian context within which I am writing. I am more familiar with the issues faced within the history of Christianity than with those of other faith traditions. However, I would hypothesize that the issues that this history highlights are to some extent generalizable to the context of other religious traditions.

Religion and Politics in the Ancient World

The first observation to make about God and politics is that in the ancient world, the present separation of religion and politics would be incomprehensible. At that time, it was inconceivable that one should separate one's national, cultural, and ethnic identity from one's religious affiliation. Indeed, they were barely distinguishable. Each people had their own gods, and in many instances political rulers were deified. The pharaohs declared themselves divine, and Roman emperors were the object of the state cult. Conquering another people meant either seeking to impose one's gods upon them or incorporating their gods into one's own religious practice. This latter approach was the Roman way, taking the gods of conquered people into their own pantheon so as to consolidate the *Pax Romana*.

One group that resisted either strategy was the Jewish people, who refused to worship the gods of foreign conquerors or to have their God represented in the pantheon of other peoples. Their resistance was in fact so fierce that they had special status within the Roman Empire, acquiring the permission to worship their God without having to take part in the Roman cult.[3] Nonetheless, Judaism remained strongly tied to one particular ethnic group. While so-called God-fearers were welcome to join them in various religious activities, they did not necessarily become Jewish. Full conversion was rare and not encouraged.

If anything, we find in the ancient world the subordination of the religious to the political order. Religion was a matter of political policy; indeed, tying the well-being of the state to religious practices was a powerful ideological tool. It legitimated the ultimate power of the state over the people, for which there was no redress, no higher

---

3. One might note their resistance to the Seleucid Empire, which sought to impose Greek gods and practices on the Jewish people, as detailed in 1–2 Maccabees.

court of appeal. State sanctions became religious sanctions; rejection of the state meant rejection of the gods and vice versa, something Socrates learned with a vengeance. Impiety was nothing less than a crime against the state. The well-being of the state was thought to depend on the maintenance of proper relationships with the gods. Heresy was treason.

This is so far from our own experience as to be almost incomprehensible to us. Religion has become such a private matter that it is hard to imagine why the state would have any interest in what I believe, apart from simply gathering information about religious practices for planning purposes.

However, these ancient practices can become more intelligible when we consider elements that have already been introduced in this work. The first observation relates to the scale of values developed in the previous chapter. Although the distinctions between values are fairly straightforward (though of course not incontestable), they are learned distinctions, often acquired over historical time frames. What we find in the ancient world is a compact appreciation of the scale of values, with little ability to distinguish vital, social, cultural, personal, and religious values. So, for example, the Old Testament law is a relatively undifferentiated mix of religious, moral, social, and hygienic norms, all under the heading of law.

The second observation relates to the distinction introduced in chapter 2 concerning cosmological and anthropological cultural types. While our present context is largely anthropological, in the ancient world the cosmological type dominated. The individual was ordered to the social and the social to the heavenly realm. The notion of individual freedom, which we take for granted, had hardly emerged in the ancient world. One's lot in life was to fit into a preexisting order provided by the social and political realm, which itself was modeled on the heavenly court.[4] One of the important features of the beginning of philosophy in ancient Greece was the ability to question these cosmological presuppositions through the injection of anthropological meanings and values. Still, this injection was met with resistance, as in the case of Socrates. So important was this anthropological breakthrough that philosopher Karl Jaspers refers to this an "Axial Age," where history itself begins to pivot.[5]

The Emergence of Religion as Distinct

While Greek philosophy marked the beginning of an emergence of anthropological meanings and values, a major change occurred as Christianity extended beyond the boundaries of Judaism. Initially, Christianity resided within Judaism as a sort of sect. However, under the impulse of its missionary mandate (Matthew 28:16-20) and the powerful vision of the apostle Paul, Christianity opened its doors to non-Jewish believers. Whatever reasons we might give for this, from the pragmatic to divine revelation, the impact was revolutionary. One's religious identity was no longer a product of one's ethnic, social, or cultural setting. As Paul summed up, there is neither Greek nor Jew, neither slave nor free, neither male nor female; all are one in Christ (Galatians 3:28). Christianity offered a religious identity that transcended all preexisting ethnic and cultural identities, not by obliterating them or replacing them, but by incorporating them within itself.[6] All that was required was faith in Christ. It has been argued that in doing so, the Christian movement "created" the category of religion. As historian Daniel Boyarin claims, "The coming of Christianity, it would seem, made the difference. The

---

4. We can see some of this fixity of social order in the caste system in India, which also reflects a cosmological ordering.

5. Karl Jaspers, *The Origin and Goal of History* (New Haven, CT: Yale University Press, 1953).

6. One finds a similar impulse in Buddhism, which transcended the boundaries of the Indus Valley to spread throughout Asia.

most dramatic innovation that Christianity introduced into the world was the making of a new kind of identity, 'religion.'"[7]

This introduction met with strong resistance, far more fierce than that encountered by Socrates. Distinguishing themselves from Jews meant the early Christians no longer enjoyed the protection offered by Jewish identity. Moreover, the ancient world could only understand their claimed allegiance to Christ as being in opposition to their loyalty to the political realm. Christianity was identified as a threat to the political order because Christians would not worship the Roman gods or take part in the cult of the emperor. They were labeled atheists and persecuted with the utmost severity; they were tortured and executed, their painful deaths on display as entertainment.[8] Thus die all enemies of the state! It is poignant to note that this first battle for a freedom we now take for granted, the freedom of religious belief without interference by the state, was fought by Christian martyrs.

Distinguishing one's religious identity from one's social and cultural identity is, however, only half the battle. Having distinguished them, how are they then intelligently related? While the ancient world placed religion at the service of the state, theoretically this was not the case for Christians. Their religious identity transcended social and cultural location in some sense. They could appeal to a different set of values; higher values that may place them in conflict with their political context. How could this be negotiated? And so we find in the writings of the early Christian apologists a defense of Christianity as not necessarily opposed to the state. Christians are actually ideal citizens, for they pray to the one

7. Daniel Boyarin, "Semantic Differences; or 'Judaism'/'Christianity,'" in *The Ways That Never Parted: Jews and Christians in Late Antiquity and the Early Middle Ages*, ed. Adam H. Becker and Annette Yoshiko Reed (Tübingen: Mohr Siebeck, 2003), 65–85, at 71.
8. On Christians being labeled atheists see Thomas S. Bokenkotter, *A Concise History of the Catholic Church*, rev. and expanded ed. (New York: Doubleday, 2004), 37.

true God for the well-being of the empire. They offer true worship and sacrifice, unlike the false worship and sacrifice of the pagans.[9] As such, they offer a more secure path toward the well-being of the empire than the pagan alternatives.

The issue was to become more complex as Christianity began to triumph over its persecutors—not through the use of force and conquest, but by persistence and patient suffering. Having spent itself in attacking Christianity, which continued to grow despite persecutions, the empire faced its own internal battles for power, with a new emperor, Constantine, emerging from the fray. For whatever reason—whether it was political pragmatism in the face of a growing population of Christians or gratitude for an apparent divine intervention at the Battle of the Milvian Bridge—Constantine took up the cause of the Christians, ceased their persecution, and offered them a special place within the empire.

While Constantine himself held to a policy of toleration toward those who continued to worship the pagan gods, later Christian emperors would not be so enlightened; they instituted their own persecution of the pagans.[10] The persecuted church became the persecuting church. In doing so, they were basically following the widespread belief of the ancient world that political unity implied and necessitated religious unity. This set the stage for the emergence of Christendom, though questions of the relationship between church and state continued to bedevil it for several centuries.

---

9. Tertullian, for example, draws attention to the fact that Christians "are ever making intercession for all the Emperors. We pray for them long life, a secure rule, a safe home, brave armies, a faithful senate, an honest people, a quiet world" (*Apology*, 30.4).

10. For a sympathetic account of Constantine and his policies toward other religions, see Peter J. Leithart, *Defending Constantine: The Twilight of an Empire and the Dawn of Christendom* (Downers Grove, IL: IVP Academic, 2010).

The Conflict of Church and State

This marriage of church and state provided ample grounds for an ongoing conflict between the two. Which was to take priority over the other? In practice, the struggle focused on what came to be called the "investiture crisis." With the collapse of the empire in the West and the emergence of feudalism, church structures were increasingly linked with the political power of feudal lords. These lords, who were not clergy, began to claim the right to appoint bishops and priests in their fiefdom. These appointments often included an oath of loyalty to the local lord. While in the early church the laity did have a role in electing people to ministry, this was a different situation altogether. Here political leaders, not the laity in general, were interfering with the autonomy of the church to appoint its own ministers, not on the basis of their suitability for the task but as an act of political patronage.

The church found the situation intolerable, and in a long and drawn-out struggle was eventually able to assert the relative superiority of religious authority over political authority.[11] The "solution" generated toward the end of the era, most fully expressed in the papal bull *Unam sanctam* (1302), was to assert (correctly) the superior value of the religious over the social ("Hence we must recognize the more clearly that spiritual power surpasses in dignity and in nobility any temporal power whatever, as spiritual things surpass the temporal"), but to infer (incorrectly, I shall argue) that this implied the right of the church to directly interfere in the political realm ("However, one sword ought to be subordinated to the other and temporal authority, subjected to spiritual power"). Yet even in this solution, the reasoning remained locked into the cosmological worldview of the old order:

11. The unedifying details can be found in any standard history of the era; for example, John A. F. Thomson, *The Western Church in the Middle Ages* (London: Arnold, 1998).

For, according to the Blessed Dionysius, it is a law of the divinity that the lowest things reach the highest place by intermediaries. Then, *according to the order of the universe*, all things are not led back to order equally and immediately, but the lowest by the intermediary, and the inferior by the superior.[12]

The cosmological form of reasoning could not be clearer. The order here below must match the heavenly order. Such reasoning no longer convinces.

While this solution temporarily resolved the dispute, things became much more complex with the breakdown of the Holy Roman Empire, the emergence of nation-states, and the beginning of the Reformation. As the emergence of the nation-state broke the fragile political unity of the empire, so the Reformation tore apart the faith unity of the church. These two fractures became mutually reinforcing, with nation-states taking different sides in various religious disputes. The old logic of the cosmological order remained in place: "*Cuius regnum eius religio*" (the state will adopt the king's religion). Political battles and religious battles merged into an era of bloody conflict, the "wars of religion."

The eventual resolution with the Peace of Westphalia continued to recognize the validity of the principle of *cuius regnum eius religio* but allowed those not of the religion of the king limited rights of worship. The emergence of religious toleration within the boundaries of a single state set the stage for the eventual breaking of the nexus between religious identity and political allegiance and the beginning of full religious pluralism in the West. This was most evident in the new United States of America, where religious freedoms were built into the constitution. This was an unprecedented step and has changed forever the ways we view church-state

---

12. All quotes from *Unam sanctam* taken from the *Internet Medieval Sourcebook*, available at http://www.fordham.edu/halsall/source/b8-unam.html. Emphasis added.

relations. While the various Protestant denominations embraced this religious freedom, in the late nineteenth century the Catholic papacy could still condemn the notion that there could be more than one religion operating within a political state.[13] The Catholic Church remained deeply suspicious of the "American experiment." Largely through the work of the American Catholic theologian John Courtney Murray, the Catholic Church eventually redefined its stance at Vatican II and began to acknowledge a right to religious freedom.[14] Now the Vatican actively appeals to this right in seeking to protect minority Christian groups in Islamic countries.

All this is by way of reminder that the "separation of church and state" is itself the product of a difficult and contentious history. The "boundaries" between church and state have been subject to constant negotiation and renegotiation over centuries, and there is no reason to think that this process of negotiation will not continue into the future. Neither religions nor states are set to disappear anytime soon. We witness some of this renegotiation today in issues such as the public wearing of the burqa in France and in secular Turkey. What are the limits of toleration in such cases? It is equally an issue when Christians seek to publically express their faith in Muslim countries. These issues regularly arise because religious communities are inherently social and cultural entities. Religious people gather together with their coreligionists, they have community events, they build churches, synagogues, temples and mosques, and because they have existed for centuries they have built up traditions of theological

13. The Syllabus of Errors condemned the notion that "The Church ought to be separated from the State, and the State from the Church" (n. 55), and lamented that "in the present day it is no longer expedient that the Catholic religion should be held as the only religion of the State, to the exclusion of all other forms of worship" (n. 77). There is also a rejection of individual freedom in matters of religion: "Every man is free to embrace and profess that religion which, guided by the light of reason, he shall consider true" (n. 15). Basically, the position was that "error has no rights."

14. On the role of John Courtney Murray, see John W. O'Malley, *What Happened at Vatican II* (Cambridge, MA: Belknap, 2008), 213–14.

and moral reflection that guide their communal life. Many of these traditions sit uneasily with the modern individualistic consumerist societies of the West. However, these Western societies have no more automatic claim to normativity than do any of the religious traditions that confront them. Negotiating boundaries may mean give and take on all sides.

Toward a Positive Proposal

I would now like to explore a proposal that would provide an alternative model for the relationship between church/religion and state, between God and politics, and that might ease the tensions in relation to a stark choice between complete secularization of the public space and Christendom/theocratic models of society. I shall initially draw out a first approximation from papal teaching on the question. I do so not because I seek to impose this as an authoritative position, but to demonstrate that some religions are taking the question seriously and are seeking to develop alternative approaches. I do not suppose that this is the only approach, but I put it forward as worthy of serious consideration. Indeed, rather than take it as simply authoritative, I shall tweak it in light of the discussion of the previous chapter on the good and the scale of values developed therein. What is significant is that this proposal does not draw on any special claims within the religious tradition, but fits neatly within the construct of a natural theology. No appeal to divine revelation or to the authority of a religious tradition will be made.

We will begin with the first encyclical of Pope Benedict XVI, *Deus caritas est*, published in 2005.[15] I want to focus on the second half of the encyclical, where Benedict develops an argument that he had

15. All quotes are taken from the Vatican website, http://www.vatican.va/holy_father/ benedict_xvi/encyclicals/documents/hf_ben-xvi_enc_20051225_deus-caritas-est_en.html.

earlier described as having "vast implications" (n. 1). Benedict starts his argument by acknowledging that "the just ordering of society and the state is a central responsibility of politics" (n. 28). By identifying justice as the "aim and intrinsic criterion of all politics," Benedict sets the stage for a discussion of the relationship between church and state, between faith and politics.

But the problem of justice is an aspect of what would traditionally be called "practical reason." How then does religious faith come into the picture? Benedict responds, "If reason is to be exercised properly, it must undergo constant purification, since it can never be completely free of the danger of a certain ethical blindness caused by the dazzling effect of power and special interests. Here faith and politics meet." In putting this case, the pope is not suggesting a direct link between faith and politics such as the Catholic Church enjoyed in the era of Christendom. In fact, he explicitly rejects the possibility of such a direct link, not once but at least four times:

1. "[Catholic social teaching] has no intention of giving the Church power over the state."
2. "It recognizes that it is not the Church's responsibility to make this teaching prevail in political life."
3. "[The Church] cannot and must not replace the state."
4. "A just society must be the achievement of politics, not of the Church." (n. 28)

These repeated affirmations make it clear that Benedict is not espousing a return to Christendom whereby the Church has some direct influence or control over the state. On the other hand, he is far from suggesting that the Church has nothing to say about the political order, or that its mission is purely "spiritual." How then does this encyclical envisage the link between faith and the political realm?

Benedict identifies a number of components to this link. He begins with an affirmation that "the Church's social teaching argues on the basis of reason and natural law, namely, on the basis of what is in accord with the nature of every human being" (n. 28). This is a strong claim, since it acknowledges that the social teaching of the Church is not grounded in revelation, the Bible, or the teaching of Christ. Rather, it is arrived at "though rational argument" (n. 28). This is in line with the type of argument developed in the previous chapter. The human good is what it is because of the type of beings we are. It is something we can come to appreciate through reflecting intelligently on our experience, without necessarily requiring a revelation from God.

The danger here is to read appeals to reason in some ahistorical or a priori way, as if the norms of reason are acknowledged and accepted by all. If this were the case, one could not mount an argument that faith can purify reason. One would either have reason or one would not, and that would be the end of the matter. But by evoking faith, which is itself a historical phenomenon, Benedict is adopting, at least implicitly, a historical account of reason. The potentialities of reason themselves unfold historically, and faith can play an important role in this unfolding process. This is particularly manifest in the Catholic Church's social teaching, which has undergone considerable historical development since the first social encyclical of Leo XIII, *Rerum novarum.*

So when Benedict speaks of "rational argument," this should not be read in some a priori sense, as if it were a deduction from given first principles, but more in the sense of engaging in dialogue, discussion, and debate on key issues over long time frames. Such a process gains greater insight and clarity as the debate continues. Further, it is through a historical account of reason that the encyclical can both claim that the Church makes "her own specific contribution towards understanding the requirements of justice and achieving them politically," and that her social teaching is not based on revelation. This is congruent with the argument of the previous chapter that the scale of values is both given by reference to human nature and also known empirically so that it emerges in traditions of moral reflection on the nature of human flourishing. Religious claims based on revelation may assist in grasping elements of the scale of values, but nonetheless they can be known apart from this as well.

The encyclical goes on to argue that through her social teaching "the Church wishes to help form consciences in political life and to stimulate greater insight into the authentic requirements of justice, as well as a greater readiness to act accordingly." While there is a sense in which this is obviously correct, there is also a sense in which some nuancing is required. If we adopt a more historical approach to the question of reason, and recognize development in the Church's social teaching, then we can also recognize that the Church's social teaching is itself a product of purified reason and formed consciences. Faith purifies reason and clarifies conscience; this has led to the development of the Church's social teaching over the past century, and prior to that in the moral area generally.

And so we have a process that moves from religious faith, to the transformation of consciences and purification of reason, to the development of a body of Church social teaching that engages our present social and cultural context. This brings us at last to the task of building a just society:

> The Church cannot and must not take upon herself the political battle to bring about the most just society possible. She cannot and must not replace the State. Yet at the same time she cannot and must not remain on the sidelines in the fight for justice. She has to play her part through rational argument and she has to reawaken the spiritual energy without which justice, which always demands sacrifice, cannot prevail and prosper. A just society must be the achievement of politics, not

of the Church. Yet the promotion of justice through efforts to bring about openness of mind and will to the demands of the common good is something which concerns the Church deeply. (n. 28)

This process of multiple mediations—from faith, to an ongoing moral conversion, to cultural engagement and rational argument, culminating in political engagement—does not lead to automatic answers at the end of the process. Indeed, over the centuries we can witness considerable development in the Catholic Church's position on a number of issues concerning the social, political order; for example, the issues of slavery, the taking of interest on loans (usury), and the value of democracy.[16]

What we see in the above analysis is an outworking of the scale of values developed in the previous chapter. Benedict is identifying, roughly speaking, a movement down the scale, from religious values, to informed consciences (personal values), to dialogue and debate (cultural values), to arrive finally at the social and political realm (social values). The primary contribution of religious values to the process is in the formation of genuinely authentic moral subjects.

This is not an exclusive claim, for authentic moral subjects can arise outside any religious tradition; nor does it specify one religious tradition over or against another; nor is it an automatic process independent of human freedom. There can be no special pleading in relation to any particular religious tradition under such a model. In the end, each must be willing to defend its contribution without appealing to elements of its religious tradition as authorities. It also places every religious tradition on notice. Nothing undermines the credibility of a religious tradition in the political realm more than the public scandal of gross immorality of its members, be it suicide bombers or sexually aberrant clergy. Again, to refer to the teaching

16. The Catholic Church was initially quite hostile to the notion of democracy but has since reconciled itself to the value of democratic processes, at least in secular society.

of Vatican II, the immorality of believers "can have more than a little to do with the birth of atheism."[17]

Political Consequences of Natural Theology

As a thought experiment, let us suppose that the existence of God is considered a publically accessible fact, something that can be derived from reasonable considerations drawn from metaphysical analysis of the success of science, the contingency of existence, and the nature of the good. Such a metaphysical framework, based on intellectual and moral conversion, may lead one to the conclusion that God does in fact exist; if successful, such a program may become culturally significant and might move us back, at least in part, to a "society where belief in God is unchallenged and indeed, unproblematic."[18] What would the consequences be for our political life?

Congruent with what I have said above, such a situation would not give preference to any one religious tradition in the political life of the nation. The conclusions of a natural theology do not distinguish between different theistic traditions. There may be an issue in relation to some nontheistic religious traditions such as Buddhism, but even here there can be flexibility. The constitution of the largely Muslim nation Indonesia, for example, takes its stand on religious monotheism—"The State shall be based upon the belief

17. More fully: "Undeniably, those who wilfully shut out God from their hearts and try to dodge religious questions are not following the dictates of their consciences, and hence are not free of blame; yet believers themselves frequently bear some responsibility for this situation. For, taken as a whole, atheism is not a spontaneous development but stems from a variety of causes, including a critical reaction against religious beliefs, and in some places against the Christian religion in particular. Hence believers can have more than a little to do with the birth of atheism. To the extent that they neglect their own training in the faith, or teach erroneous doctrine, or are deficient in their religious, moral or social life, they must be said to conceal rather than reveal the authentic face of God and religion." *Gaudium et Spes*, n. 19 available at http://www.vatican.va/archive/hist_councils/ii_vatican_council/documents/vat-ii_cons_19651207_gaudium-et-spes_en.html.
18. Charles Taylor, *A Secular Age* (Cambridge, MA: Belknap, 2007), 3.

in the One and Only God" (Article 29 [1])[19]—but the government recognizes six "monotheistic" religions: Islam, Protestantism, Catholicism, Hinduism, Confucianism, *and* Buddhism. Freedom of religion is guaranteed by the constitution, but freedom from religion is not recognized. While we may demur on this last point, it does indicate that public recognition of God's existence does not imply a theocratic conclusion, with only one religious tradition calling the shots, even where one group is significantly more numerous than the others. There can be public respect for diverse religious traditions in a state that recognizes the existence of God.

One may push the argument further and ask whether the state should actively support religious traditions. Certainly, one tradition should not be favored over another, at least not on the basis of a natural theology. However, one can argue that the worship of God in gratitude for existence is a moral imperative for all people that the state may recognize and support, even if this support is the minimal support of tax-exempt status for religious organizations or similar arrangements. In fact, we find such recognition and support in many states already.

On the other hand, religious traditions cannot expect an appeal to the specifics of their beliefs, which go beyond what is available through a natural theology, to be authoritative in their contributions to public debate. They can appeal to whatever metaphysical reasoning may develop as a consequence of intellectual and moral conversion in relation to particular contentious issues such as abortion or euthanasia, but they must recognize that on such matters even their coreligionists might not agree completely. Their task is to engage in the type of rational debate suggested by Benedict XVI, to enlarge the cultural resources made available through intellectual and

19. *The 1945 Constitution of the Republic of Indonesia*, available at http://www.embassyofindonesia.org/about/pdf/IndonesianConstitution.pdf.

moral conversion to enable a growing consensus on such matters. But still we might expect that "it happens rather frequently, and legitimately so, that with equal sincerity some [believers] will disagree with others on a given matter."[20]

The practical outcome of the proposal above is one of constant negotiation and renegotiation of the boundaries between, and issues relating to, church and state. One can expect the boundaries to be regularly tested on a variety of issues—like same-sex marriage, tax-free status, anti-discrimination legislation, and health care provisions—on which religious communities must be able to mount a reasonable account of their position that does not rely solely on claimed revelation. What is not acceptable from the perspective of a natural theology is direct political engagement through the formation of movements or parties that claim to represent the political embodiment of a religious tradition, even in a situation where that religious tradition might constitute the majority of the population of a nation. This would bypass multiple mediations—from religious faith, to personal authenticity, to cultural transformation leading to political outcomes—in an attempt to draw a direct line from the religious to the political. It attempts to give religious or even divine authority to what are often contentious political outcomes even within the community of believers. While identifying their political stance with their religious convictions is a constant temptation for religious communities, it carries with it dangers for both the religious community and for the political order.

20. *Gaudium et Spes*, n. 43.

The Unhappy Alliance of the Political
and Religious Orders

In the alliance of the political and religious orders, the dangers for the political order are the more obvious and most often encountered. The granting of religious authority to a political order gives the political order an absolute authority and power that is unacceptable for it to hold. Political decisions are matters of practical intelligence, and in the realm of the practical there is always a proviso of "best decision given present knowledge" or "best decision given realizable outcomes" that simply does not admit of the certainty of religious belief. Attempts to give such outcomes the weight of religious authority seek to shut down the political process of debate and negotiation by ruling out any contrary opinion. These attempts claim a level of certainty that the political realm can never achieve. The absolutism of such positions is terrifying in its far-reaching consequences. As conservative commentator Michael Novak suggests, "Even philosopher kings, given total power, may sooner or later be tempted to torture others. . . . Some pretext is always at hand."[21]

Many (though not all) of the objections raised by Christopher Hitchens in his book *God Is Not Great* relate to this unhappy collapsing of the scale of values whereby the political and religious orders merge. As Hitchens documents, all major religious traditions have failed in this regard. We see it in the clashes between Catholics and Protestants in Northern Ireland, in Hindu nationalism in India, and in the political aspirations of Islamic jihadists. Christians, Muslims, Jews, Hindus, and Buddhists all fall under his lash with

---

21. Michael Novak, *Will It Liberate? Questions about Liberation Theology* (New York: Paulist Press, 1986), 200–201.

examples of this unholy alliance between religious belief and political process.

Yet while one may agree that these are unacceptable outcomes, one may also reject the diagnosis that religion itself is the problem. Any good thing can be misused, including religion. And its misuse has seriously bad consequences precisely because evil is parasitic on the good, and the greater the good involved, the greater the possible evil that can emerge in its distortion. The solution lies not in eliminating religion but in vigilance. Both the political realm and religious communities must be on their guard against such distortions.

However, there are also disadvantages for religious communities in the alliance of the political and religious orders. The imprecision of the political order, the variability and often unpredictability of its outcomes, the occurrence of events beyond anyone's control particularly in regard to economic matters, can affect religious authority. Political and economic failures reflect badly on the authority of the religious tradition, with ordinary believers losing faith in their tradition. It can become very evident that religious authority cannot provide the needed solutions to a problem in garbage collection, or unpaved roads, or a failure in hospital services, and so on, let alone a major economic crisis engendered by global forces beyond the control of national political leadership.[22]

The question religious communities need to face is whether they are willing to risk the weight of religious authority on such unpredictable and uncontrollable outcomes. Why would one want to wager religious authority on the ability of politicians to get the trains to run on time? Religious authority cannot supply answers to all the problems faced in running a political system, particularly one

---

22. I have read news reports of such things occurring in Iran, where poor political outcomes have reflected badly on the religious leadership, leading people to question religious authority.

as complex as a modern state. It is naïve and somewhat infantile to think that it can. Such naïveté can rapidly spill over into violence when expectations in the political order are not achieved. People will be blamed for not trying hard enough, for lacking faith, for not trusting in God sufficiently, and so on. These trajectories are all too common and should be known to all. There is nothing to be gained from religious communities going down this path. In the end, it gives religion a bad name and brings religious belief into disrepute.

Repentance for Past Failures

All this has not stopped religious movements in the past, nor is it likely to stop further attempts in the future. The solution on the side of religions may be to begin to acknowledge the history of past failures and not to romanticize or idealize the past. Christendom in the West was not an ideal period that we should long to return to. It was a failed political experiment that proved unstable and unworkable in the long run. It is not a model to be repeated. Similarly, one can have some intellectual assurance that present experiments in theocracy, in Iran for example, will prove equally unstable and unworkable. Given the rapid rate of social and technological change and the mass communications available, together with increasing global connectedness, such modern experiments are unlikely to last for centuries as did Christendom. Their lifetime is more likely to be measured in decades.

Rather than romanticizing and idealizing such experiments, they should be viewed as past sins that evoke repentance. Here all religions could do well to reflect on the example set by Pope John Paul II at the turn of the new millennium. Faced with a history of institutional failures, the pope formally asked for forgiveness for the Catholic Church's sins: sins committed in service of the truth where the church "sometimes used methods not in keeping with the Gospel in the solemn duty of defending the truth"; sins against the unity of the church that have "rent the unity of the Body of Christ and wounded fraternal charity"; sins against the people of Israel, thereby acknowledging the complicity of the Church in anti-Semitism; sins arising from a failure to respect the cultures and religions of others "caused by pride, by hatred and a desire to dominate others"; sins against the dignity of women ("who are all too often humiliated and emarginated") and against the unity of humankind; and sins against the fundamental rights of persons, "especially for minors who are victims of abuse, for the poor, the alienated, the disadvantaged."[23] Such an act of repentance should rob any religious community of triumphalist pretensions in the political order.

A Non-Tribal God?

One of the advantages of building the case for God on the basis of a natural theology is that it makes very clear that God is not a tribal god belonging to one people, one race, or one nation. This is a God who creates the entire universe, who is the source of all being and all goodness; we cannot evoke God against the other as if they are excluded from God's care, because they, too, are known and loved into existence by this one true God. This God places the same moral demands on all people and stands in opposition to all evil, particularly evil perpetrated in God's name, which is the ultimate betrayal of all that God is. God cannot ask anyone to do an immoral deed, thereby magically turning evil into good. This God cannot be evoked to destroy one's enemies; this God will not bring down fire from heaven in vengeance or retribution. Rather, God makes the sun shine and the

23. The full text is available at http://www.vatican.va/news_services/liturgy/documents/ ns_lit_doc_20000312_prayer-day-pardon_en.html.

rain fall on the good and the bad alike. God's sanctions against human wickedness can extend beyond the present life far more powerfully than any human sanctions. In particular, God does not need us to defend the divine honor.

None of this should suggest that God cannot, or has not, acted within human history to address particular people, races, or nations. But it is to suggest that where we draw conclusions from such acts of divine election that contradict the outcomes of a sound natural theology, then we must look again at those conclusions and question their validity. For example, the Bible portrays God as changing the divine mind, but the present natural theology argues that God is unchanging. Which way should we go? The Bible may portray God as sanctioning violent immoral acts. Should we take this at face value? And so, from the church's earliest centuries, Christian thinkers recognized the need to purify their faith in the light of good philosophy, to eliminate anthropomorphic understandings of God, and reinterpret such passages in ways congruent with what reason required.[24] The Bible may speak of God's right hand, but we would be foolish to suggest God has a body with a right and left hand, just like us.

This is particularly important in the current context, where fundamentalist and literalist readings of religious tradition based on particular claims to divine revelation often stand in contradiction to the outcomes of reason, be it scientific, moral, or metaphysical. Worse still, these claims take on a tribal dimension of "our god against your god" (or your godlessness). Natural theology resists all such claims because it understands God as the source of all meaning, all truth, and all goodness, wherever it is found. For religion to

24. For example, Clement of Alexandria warned of the dangers of anthropomorphizing God on the basis of the biblical text. See Bernard J. F. Lonergan, "The Absence of God in Modern Culture," in *A Second Collection*, ed. William Ryan and Bernard Tyrell (Philadelphia: Westminster, 1974), 101–16, at 109.

contradict reason would then be for God to contradict Godself. That way lies madness.

Conclusion

In this chapter, we have explored some of the issues that arise in relation to natural theology and the political realm. While an accepted natural theology precludes an agenda of aggressive secularization, it does not sanction the claims of a theocracy or a return to Christendom. Rather, it can allow us to see the flaws in such a political accommodation of religion. Further, not only does this rejection of such totalizing claims lead to better politics, it also frees religions from the inevitable difficulties that arise in the political order. Religious faith cannot make the trains run on time, nor should it be the concern of religious authorities to make it so. Neither does a natural theology sanction the imposition of irrationalism onto the public domain, where religious beliefs are presented in a naïve, fundamentalist or literalist way. It can act to purify those beliefs inside the religious tradition and thus assist in bringing the concerns of faith into public debate.

All of this remains hypothetical; we are far from having such a public acknowledgement of God's existence, especially in the increasingly secular West. Whether such a large-scale cultural shift is feasible is a difficult question. Nonetheless, it is important to recognize that these are important issues for natural theology to address. In the final chapter, we will turn our attention to the most controverted natural theological issue of all: that of theodicy. How can there be a good God in the face of so much suffering and evil?

7

God and the Problems of Pain, Suffering, and Evil

We now come to the final and most difficult topic to deal with in any natural theology: the problems of pain, suffering, and evil. For many people, these are the knockdown arguments against the traditional understanding of God as benevolent, omniscient, and omnipotent. In the light of human suffering and evil, either God is not good (because God does nothing to address the problem), or if God is good, God is not omnipotent (because the problem remains). Or perhaps God does not know, in which case God is not omniscient.

And the problem is rarely just a philosophical one. Underneath such questioning there can be a very real existential bite. It is an uncommon life that is not touched in some significant way by pain, suffering, or evil. Often, the question is not, "Why is there suffering?" but "Why did this loved one suffer?" or "Why did this evil befall me?"

In chapter 2, I noted that the metaphysical undertaking may require certain intellectual and moral dispositions. Just as a scientist requires training in the scientific method and must learn to appreciate the value of intellectual honesty to resist temptations to falsify data, so too metaphysicians may require certain intellectual and moral dispositions to be successful in their undertakings. In chapter 3 and chapter 5, these dispositions were further specified in terms of intellectual and moral conversion. Without intellectual conversion, it is impossible to resist the myth of the real as the already-out-there-now reality of extroverted animal consciousness, with its persistent reductionism that is always looking for smaller and smaller things as the "building blocks" for all reality. Without intellectual conversion, our human world of meanings and values is mere illusion. Intellectual and moral conversions allow us to affirm the reality and intelligibility of values and to specify a normative hierarchy of values. Without these two conversions, the theodicy problem—the "justification" of God in the face of the problems of pain, suffering, and evil—is intractable. With these conversions in place, we can begin to map out a response that is congruent with the account of God developed in the present work.

Some Basic Distinctions

Above I spoke of "pain, suffering, and evil," implying that these are three distinct categories. It is now time to justify such an implication. The bases for the distinctions are already to be found in previous chapters.

First, let us consider the issue of pain. In chapter 4, I noted the matter of consciousness as a property of animal existence that allows for a greater responsiveness to the animal's habitat. An animal is consciously oriented to find food and water (feelings of hunger and thirst), to mate (instinctive sex drive), and so on. Through its eyes and ears, it can detect prey for the hunt or predators to flee; through taste, it can distinguish good things to eat from poisons and other harmful material. However, it can also experience pain as the body's warning system that something is wrong. Pain demands our attention and appropriate action. Without pain, animals may lead a pain-free life, but it might also be a short life. In this sense, the ability to experience pain is a good thing. While never pleasant, the experience of pain is the intelligible outcome of the body's need to know when it is in danger and is required to take action to protect itself. In terms of the scale of values, then, pain is a vital value. Its occurrence is a good thing because it prompts appropriate action.

From a more metaphysical perspective, pain occurs when a finite conscious being reaches limits, whether those limits are physical (the breaking of bones from forces beyond their tensile strength), chemical (the presence of poisons, which disrupt the normal biochemical cycles in our cells), biological (the presence of viruses or bacteria, which subvert our biological processes for their own reproduction) or psychological (overwhelming stress arising from our situation or context). Pain informs us that we have reached or are already beyond our limits. To be a finite conscious being is to be able to experience pain and is, in all likelihood, to actually experience it at some time. From this perspective, the "solution" to the problem of pain is either not to be conscious or not to be finite—that is, to have no limits. To not be conscious would not be a very interesting form of existence, while to have no limits would make one nothing less than God.[1]

Second, there is the problem of suffering. We may distinguish pain from suffering by reference to the question of meaning. People can endure pain when there is some meaning or purpose to it. And so

---

1. The problem of pain is often referred to as the problem of "natural evil." I prefer not to refer to this as evil per se inasmuch as pain is perfectly intelligible as arising from our biological nature, especially in an evolutionary context. As such it operates as a vital good, however uncomfortable or unpleasant it may be.

we might endure the pain of surgery and its consequent recovery as a better alternative to dying from cancer. I can endure the stretches and strains of physiotherapy since I know it will alleviate my lower back problems. A woman may endure the pain of childbirth because of the meaning of the new life that emerges. However, there is also the problem of chronic pain, or constant high levels of pain for which there is no relief, or pain imposed by another for no good reason. Such a situation can lead to a crisis of meaning or purpose. Thus we might think of suffering as pain that precipitates a crisis of meaning or purpose. This is a particularly human experience because meaning is central to human living.

This human dimension of meaning leads to a different solution to the problem of suffering. While I have argued above that pain itself is inherently linked to the issue of finite conscious existence, and so has a basic meaning, nonetheless it can so invade consciousness as to seriously impair our quest to construct a meaningful and purposeful life. Under some circumstances, life can then appear "meaningless." However, if the problem of suffering concerns a crisis of meaning, the solution involves addressing how one might make or discover meaning within one's suffering. Sometimes the problem can be alleviated by discovering a hidden meaning, such as the diagnosis of a disease that can then be treated and the pain removed. Knowing there is a cause and a solution can help make pain more endurable. However, more often than not the solution is not one of discovering meaning, but of creating meaning. A person who is suffering from some chronic pain may gather together other people with a similar issue and create a community that helps one another to find common practical solutions to their condition. The very act of organizing, of bringing people together, can create a new meaning that helps to alleviate the suffering, if not the pain, of the chronic condition. Similarly, some victims of crime might work for greater justice, through changes in the law, to help minimize the possibility of the same thing happening to others. While the pain of loss may remain, the suffering is alleviated by the creation of this meaningful outcome to a bad situation.

Finally, there is the issue of evil. I noted in chapter 5 that the problem of evil properly arises in the context of the human responsibility to act according to the dictates of intelligence and reason. Evil arises in the human failure to live according to the purpose of human existence. It occurs when we act without good or proper reasons for acting, such as when we act to achieve a lower-order value when a higher-order value is attainable and in conflict with the lower-order value. So, for example, I may run away from the enemy attacking my country; I have protected my own vital value, but not arisen to protect the good of order for my nation. I may gain economic and political power (social value) but be corrupted morally (personal value) into thinking that the normal moral rules of human behavior, such as marital fidelity, no longer apply to me.

The problem of evil is fundamentally different from the problem of pain. While there are perfectly intelligible reasons why pain occurs, given our finite and biological constitution, evil arises when we act unintelligently, unreasonably, and irresponsibly. While there is a statistical inevitability to pain, there is no such inevitability to evil.

Suffering, on the other hand, may be the outcome of evil. Where evil causes pain, it does so without proper purpose or reason, and so it leads to a crisis of meaning in the person who experiences the pain. Suffering as a crisis of meaning may also become a context for evil in us when our suffering induces us to act unintelligently, unreasonably, and irresponsibly. Our suffering may provide a context or excuse for our failed action, but it does not amount to a good reason.

This lack of meaningfulness extends beyond individuals and reaches into the ways in which we organize our society and the cultural meanings and values we develop to justify those ways. And so an individual may disparage a person whose skin is a different color from their own with little impact beyond their own circle of activity, but such attitudes can become institutionalized in political and economic systems that exclude people of color from economic and political power, justified on the basis that such people are "inherently inferior." Our social and cultural orders become distorted carriers of the meaninglessness of racism, such that it becomes the air we breathe, the presupposition of our activities. Evil then becomes the norm to which we are expected to conform and from which we must struggle to free ourselves.

Is there, then, a solution to this problem of evil? I shall address this later in the chapter. In the meantime, however, I will note that the distinctions above are intelligible and reasonable. It is a mistake to try to lump them together or to fail to note their distinctiveness. Nonetheless, many authors tend to do so. A scientific reductionist has enough of a problem acknowledging the reality of consciousness, let alone the reality of meaning or of the moral imperatives implicit in reason. If consciousness is not real, then pain is an illusion; suffering as distinct from pain makes little sense; and to distinguish evil from pain and suffering is unintelligible. But even a scientific reductionist knows well enough to visit a dentist when she has a toothache (vital value) and to live according to the obligations of civil society (social value). She will seek to promote the scientific method (cultural value) and rightly rails against a scientist who falsifies data (personal value). A reductionist's account of morality rarely conforms to the performative morality of our living.

More disturbing, however, is the failure of some Christian apologists to make these basic distinctions. And so Stewart Goetz begins his discussion of theodicy with the declaration, "First, the problem of evil is fundamentally, in the words of C. S. Lewis, the problem of pain (Lewis 1962), where an experience of pain is an irreducible, conscious feeling or quale that hurts."[2] Whether this is an adequate account of the position of C. S. Lewis I shall leave others to judge. But as a starting point for discussing the problem of evil, it is clearly inadequate. When one begins to mount, for example, a "free will defense" theodicy, arguing that the existence of evil is somehow justified by the goodness of free will, one should hopefully note that such a defense leaves the problem of pain untouched. There is no logical connection between the existence of free will and the existence of pain; there was pain in the animal kingdom well before the imperative to be responsible, with its appeal to human freedom. Also, one can do quite wicked things without causing any pain as such. A financial swindle may go under the radar of investors, skimming off a low level of profit, without causing any "pain" to the investors as "an irreducible, conscious feeling or quale that hurts."[3] Further, we don't put humans down like animals when they suffer, as if alleviating their suffering means eliminating evil in their lives. To do so against their will would be tantamount to murder. Much of the force of the euthanasia debate comes from our cultural assumption that pain is the greatest evil we can encounter.

2. Stewart Goetz, "The Argument from Evil," in *The Blackwell Companion to Natural Theology*, ed. William Lane Craig and J. P. Moreland (Oxford: Blackwell, 2009), 449. The internal reference is to C. S. Lewis, *The Problem of Pain* (New York: HarperOne, 2001). To be fair to Goetz, many who engage in theodicy seem to regularly blur these distinctions.

3. A good example of this was a bank swindle in which a computer operator skimmed off all the fractions of a cent that were regularly rounded down in various interest calculations and accumulated them into a personal account. While each amount was very small, given the larger number of transactions the account amassed a large sum of money. It was doubtful anyone felt any "pain" in the ingenious process, yet it was clearly immoral.

Intellectual and Moral Conversion
and the Problem of Evil

The distinctions above between pain, suffering, and evil take their stand on moral and intellectual conversion.

Moral conversion means moving away from satisfactions and dissatisfactions as our basic criteria for decision making and moving toward genuine values and disvalues. Pleasure and pain generate satisfactions (pleasure) and dissatisfactions (pain), but as we have seen above, pain can be viewed as a vital value. The presence or absence of pain is not a criterion for making a decision of itself without asking, first, What is the meaning of this pain? What does it signify? Its meaning then indicates the type of decision that needs to be made. For example, one might be willing to put up with some measure of pain in order to achieve higher-level values. An athlete might need to break through the pain barrier in order to achieve social recognition and success (social value). A person may endure torture yet maintain some level of personal integrity (personal value) by not betraying secrets to the enemy. Indeed, the person might even be willing to die rather than betray such secrets. Similarly, pleasure of a sexual nature might correlate with certain vital values—the release of tension, a lowering of blood pressure, and so on—all of which add to one's vital well-being. However, such pleasures need to be integrated into a meaningful and purposeful life, not just pursued endlessly for their own sake. Obeying Dawkins's injunction to "enjoy your own sex lives"[4] could involve a narcissistic masturbatory fantasy life rather than a life that involves the realities of relationship, commitment, and fidelity. Pleasure pursued for its own sake is hardly a guide to moral living but more like a recipe for addiction.

4. Richard Dawkins, *The God Delusion* (London: Bantam, 2006), 264.

While moral conversion plays an important part in helping to distinguish issues of pain, suffering, and evil, the more decisive contribution comes from intellectual conversion. Intellectual conversion allows us to assert the reality of values, and so helps consolidate moral conversion. However, and more importantly, the criteria of intelligibility and reasonableness that intellectual conversion brings in relation to knowing reality provide an important metaphysical insight into the nature of evil. To spell this out, we can return to the story of Augustine's intellectual conversion in Book 7 of *The Confessions*. We have already seen how Augustine provides a narrative of his own shift, contrasting his naïve position, which identified reality as already-out-there-now, with his later position implicit in Nebridius's reasoned argument against Manichaeism.

This shift in his understanding of the nature of reality provides Augustine with a different way to approach the problem of evil. Now existence is linked with reason. Everything that exists has its reasons for existence—reasons that ultimately relate to its existence from God. Everything that exists is therefore good, because God wills it to be. Evil, on the other hand, "cannot be a substance," and "for you [God] evil has no being at all."[5] These denials are not a solution to the problem of evil that tries to merely think evil out of existence. If we were still in a world where reality is the "already-out-there-now" real that Augustine is rejecting, this would be the case. To say that evil has no substance or being would be to eliminate it from space and time. But this is not Augustine's meaning. If reality, substance, and existence correlate with reason, then unreality, lack of substance, and nonexistence are the antithesis of reason. What Augustine is stating when he says evil has no substance is that evil has no reasons. It lacks

---

5. Augustine, *The Confessions*, trans. Maria Boulding (New York: Vintage Books, 1998), 174–75.

that which is constitutive of reality, that is, sufficient reason. Evil is thus a privation of the good, the good of sufficient reason to be.

Wherein lies this lack of reason? Primarily in human willing where we act with insufficient or poor reasons. Augustine has already prepared us for this conclusion in Book 2 of *The Confessions*, in the story where he and some friends stole some pears, only to then throw them against a wall. There Augustine scrutinizes his childhood misdemeanor with a penetrating interrogation as to his motives for his action. He begins his account with a blunt acknowledgment that his action had "*no reason . . .* there was *no motive* for my malice except malice."[6] Indeed, the whole analysis of his and others' actions revolves around the notion of motivation, or reasons for one's actions. "People look for *the reason* why some criminal act has been committed."[7] In his critical self-examination, he finds "nothing": "I found nothing to love save the theft itself."[8] In the end, he finds his own actions unintelligible: "Who understands his faults?"[9] This lack of reasonable motivation or intelligibility for the act is the psychological correlate of Augustine's metaphysical analysis of evil as lacking substance.

This is the decisive metaphysical breakthrough concerning the nature of evil. Evil is not some "thing" in the world of the already-out-there-now reality of extroverted consciousness. Evil is rather a privation, a lack, something missing that should be there but isn't. Its primary locus is the subject, the one who acts unintelligently, unreasonably, and irresponsibly. Its consequences are often more obvious in the harm, the suffering caused to others, but not necessarily. The real evil is *primarily* the damage done to the subject who fails to be what a human being is meant to be, and *secondarily*

6. Ibid., 68.
7. Ibid., 69.
8. Ibid., 72.
9. Ibid., 73.

the damage done to the victims of the failed decision. Now, to be a victim of evil is to face a serious moral challenge: How do I respond? Do I forgive or strike back? Seek vengeance? Retribution? Justice? Suffer in silence? However, the failed human being has few options. One can remain locked into ever-tighter cycles of self-justification for one's irresponsible decision,[10] or one takes up the path of genuine repentance and seeks to make reparation to one's victims.

Without intellectual conversion, we inevitably tend to think of evil either in terms of its most obvious consequences (pain and suffering) or in terms of some "thing," or positive quality of things, and so we tend toward a dualist account of evil. To focus on the most obvious consequences is another version of the real issue being "out there now" in the pain and suffering of the victim. Intellectual conversion pushes us deeper into the intelligibility (or lack thereof) of the actions that give rise to the consequences. This problem of dualism raises another concern, and to address this trajectory we need to consider God in relation to the problem of evil.

God and the Problem of Evil

As noted at the beginning of this chapter, the problem of evil is often seen as an argument against the existence of a divine omnipotent and benevolent being. However, if one accepts the sorts of arguments presented in this current work, the problem is far more radical than the atheist stance could imagine. Take the argument from contingent being: God is the cause of all contingent being. Evil is a contingent occurrence. It is not necessitated or self-explanatory; hence it is contingent. And so God is the cause of all evil. This would be a

---

10. Often the best rationalization is to repeat the act. If it was right once, it will be right a second time and a third time, and so on. Sin then takes on the qualities of an addiction, as Augustine well knew.

devastating blow to religious belief. How can such a conclusion be avoided?

One common and simple solution that is found in some religious traditions is to posit a second source of being, distinct from God, who is responsible for evil, so that both good and evil are equiprimordial. God is the source of all goodness, and an anti-God—Satan or the devil—is responsible for all evil. The whole of creation is then a contest or battle between forces of good and evil. This is the classical expression of dualism as found in Manichaeism, a position that the young Augustine held for a number of years before his conversion to Christianity. Often this is expressed as a dualism of spirit and matter, with spirit good and matter evil. It is attractive in its simplicity, but in the end Augustine recognized that it left goodness powerless in the face of evil. In dualism, the fact of evil is built into the ontological structure of reality; it is as pointless to rail against it as it is to rail against the existence of the sun. One must either live with it or seek a position "beyond good and evil," whatever that might mean. In fact, such a dualism was precisely the target of Nebridius's argument that Augustine and his friends found irrefutable.

Yet if we reject this dualism, how do we avoid placing evil at the feet of God as the cause of all contingent reality? Here again Augustine's insight into the nature of evil as without substance is the major breakthrough. The nature of evil is revealed as the lack of sufficient reason. Given that reason should be the basic cause of human actions, to act with a lack of reason is to lack a sufficient cause for one's actions. Evil is therefore uncaused. It is the gap between what is and what should have been that occurs because a person acts without sufficient cause (reason). If evil is characterized by this lack of cause, then God cannot be the cause of evil either. In more modern parlance, we might speak of evil as a lack of meaning in, or the meaninglessness of, an action. Something about the action resists our ability to comprehend it. Again, as the source of all meaning, God is not the source of meaninglessness. Not even God understands evil, because in a real sense there is nothing there to be understood. This stance refuses to put good and evil on the same ontological basis. They are not equiprimordial; rather, evil is parasitic on the good. It feeds off and distorts the good. Good can exist without evil, but evil depends on the good to exist.

This also reveals the radical nature of evil. My primary position in this work has been the intelligibility of the real. Evil seeks to undo the order of creation by "creating" unintelligibility, by unpicking the threads of meaning that hold reality together. Where the purpose of human action is to expand the field of meaning, truth, and goodness, the occurrence of evil sows meaninglessness, mendacity, and privation. Evil is anti-creation. However, it can never claim for itself the intelligibility of the real; rather, it is a pseudo-reality that resists all our efforts at understanding.[11] As such, it is not just a human failure to be what we are meant to be; it is an offense against God and God's creation. It is sin.

Why Does God Permit Pain, Suffering, and Evil?

The question then arises, If God is the creator of all contingent being, why does God create a world in which there is pain, suffering, and evil? Given that we have drawn an intelligible distinction between these three, one would not expect there to be a single answer to cover all together.

As noted above, pain is a consequence of our having a finite, conscious nature. It is a biological mechanism that serves to protect

---

11. It is wonderfully captured in the film *The Neverending Story*, when one of the characters proclaims that "a strange sort of Nothing is destroying everything." The Nothing defies positive description. The author clearly has an Augustinian metaphysics of evil in mind.

us from greater harm. Once we reach our limits, we experience pain. The only ways of avoiding pain are to either be unconscious (like a tree, for example: alive but unresponsive) or to not be finite, to have no limits. But only God has no limits whatsoever. It would seem, then, that the possibility of pain is constitutive of any finite creation with conscious creatures. God could have made a universe in which consciousness did not emerge, but it would not have been a very interesting place. In fact, there would have been no one around to find it interesting or uninteresting since "interest" is a conscious state. On the other hand, consciousness is good and allows for much more varied forms of existence, including human existence with a consciousness oriented to meaning, truth, and goodness. Especially when we take the millions of years of evolution into account and all the pain of the animal kingdom "red in tooth and claw," some might feel that the emergence of consciousness was not worth the price. Nonetheless, the ability to ask such a question and the possibility of answering it depend on the emergence of consciousness itself. To repudiate the conditions from which we have emerged is to repudiate our own existence.

The problem of suffering is a distinctively human problem because it concerns a crisis of meaning that arises from prolonged or purposeless suffering. It poses a particularly moral challenge to us because of the temptation it produces to act in ways that are less than intelligent, reasonable, and responsible. There is also the distress such situations can cause loved ones who must witness such suffering in us. Nonetheless, it is only one moral challenge among many we all face in life, like the temptation to cheat on our spouse, to embezzle money from our employer, to live a dissolute life devoid of purpose while entertaining ourselves to death, and so on. The problem of suffering is just one such challenge. Should God have created a world in which there are no moral challenges? Such moral challenges, including suffering, can and have become an occasion for heroic virtue whereby people create meaning from their situation, displaying courage and hope, patience and forbearance, and even trust in God's providence and love.[12] Of course, none of this means we should not act to reduce a person's suffering through appropriate medical care, just as we can work to reduce other temptations in our lives. No sane person seeks out a life of suffering, but reasonable people can expect to encounter times of genuine suffering in their life and should be prepared to face the moral challenges it presents.[13]

Finally, we come to the problem of evil. Asking why God allows evil is problematic, since I have argued above that God is not the cause of evil. Not even God understands why evil occurs, because there is no intelligibility, no reason for its occurrence; it is the very absence of sufficient intelligibility and reason that defines an act as evil.[14] To ask why God permits evil sounds like God gives permission for evil to occur. In fact, God repudiates evil; God forbids evil. God creates us as intelligent, reasonable, and responsible, with the expectation that these imperatives will guide our actions. If called to account for our lives, we cannot turn to God and say, "But you permitted evil." So we might reframe the question as, "Why does God create a world in which evil occurs?"

Theologically, this is getting closer to the mark. God's act of creation is sovereign and free. God could have chosen to create any

---

12. Some theodicies refer to this as "soul-making"; for example, John Hick, *Evil and the God of Love* (London: Macmillan, 1966), 289–97. Hick traces this type of theodicy back to the second-century church father Irenaeus.

13. One of the traps of the religious life is the irrational expectation that somehow being religious will protect us from suffering. There is nothing in any major religious tradition that would make such a claim, but often religious people are shocked when they encounter suffering. "Why me? I've been good. Why is God doing this to me?" and so on. The religious life cannot and does not protect us from suffering. It can, however, when genuinely engaged, provide a source of grace to prevent us falling into the temptations that arise when suffering occurs.

14. This is no more a limit on God's omniscience or omnipotence than saying God cannot find a rational number whose square is two. What is unintelligible by definition cannot be understood, even by God. Neither can God make the unintelligible intelligible by divine fiat.

number of universes, but of all possible universes this is the one God has created. Of course, God could have chosen a universe in which freedom never arose, and so the problem of evil did not occur. But in other ways such a universe would have been defective. There equally would have been no creatures who could have reflected on the intelligibility and reasonableness of the universe, to have plumbed its depths in science, to have explored its meaning and purpose in philosophy and theology, or reflected its beauty in art. These are good things and perhaps worth the risk. Could God not have chosen a universe in which beings exist who are intelligent, reasonable, and responsible, like us, but who never actually sinned, though they were capable of sinning? We cannot dismiss such a possibility. There is no necessity in sin, no reason for it, so such an outcome is not self-contradictory. But we know that this is not the universe God chose to create. And so we might ask whether we can gain some insight into why God may have so chosen.

Clearly, the occurrence of evil "ups the ante" in terms of the problem of suffering. It adds pain that is unjustly imposed by another to the chronic or excessive pain that arises from natural causes. Being a victim of another's sin imposes an added moral challenge. How do I respond to such an imposition? And what are the options available for the sinner? However, there also emerges the possibility of new forms of the good that are not found in a universe where there is no evil: the mutually related goods of forgiveness and repentance. These change the dynamics of the moral life, adding complexity, but also a beauty not found in a morally perfect situation. Still, one may ask whether it has been worth it. Is God's choice of this universe worth the history of human evil that continually threatens to engulf us, the horrendous evils we have witnessed, particularly in the last century, and with the current threat of irreversible human-caused climate change with its disastrous consequences for future generations? Perhaps the answer to this lies beyond the scope of a purely natural theology. As Bernard Lonergan has suggested:

> Without faith, without the eye of love, the world is too evil for God to be good, for a good God to exist. But faith recognizes that God grants men their freedom, that he wills them to be persons and not just his automata, that he calls them to the higher authenticity that overcomes evil with good.[15]

However, one must be very clear that the emergence of forgiveness and repentance do not amount to a justification or reason for the occurrence of evil in God's creation. They are a response to the unintelligibility of evil, not a justification for its occurrence. Evil remains evil, without cause or reason, but it becomes the opportunity for new good to emerge.

One may push the issue of evil further. We have considered new forms of good that can emerge in relation to evil. This remains, however, at a human level of response. The larger question is, Can we conceive of God responding to evil? Is there a divinely originated solution to the problem of evil in which human beings are invited to participate? If so, how might we recognize such a possibility?

A Divinely Originated Solution to the Problem of Evil

One of the paradoxes of the dualist account of the problem of evil is that the solution to the problem is both simple and impossible. It is simple because if evil is substantial, some "thing," then the solution to the problem of evil is to corral the evil and fence it off, and perhaps even to attempt to destroy it with whatever means one has at one's disposal. This is often the logic of a dualist political rhetoric, which labels the enemy evil (or perhaps an "axis of evil") and so any

---

15. Bernard J. F. Lonergan, *Method in Theology* (London: DLT, 1972), 117.

means of destroying that evil is then justified.[16] However, the solution is impossible in the sense that evil is understood as an ontological constituent of reality. In the end, it cannot be eliminated; good and evil are locked in an eternal conflict that can never be resolved.

On the other hand, the account of evil as privation of the good—as a lack of intelligibility, reasonableness, and responsibility—refuses to provide a theoretical solution to the problem of evil, something that would incorporate evil into the intelligibility of the whole, but it does point the way toward a practical solution to the problem.[17] That solution is to take the occurrence of evil as an opportunity to create a new intelligibility and reasonableness through the exercise of greater responsibility. Out of the nonbeing of evil, we create a new reality that seeks to overcome the consequences of the original occurrence.

Such a process is likely to be a form of suffering. Evil may be a cause of suffering, as noted above, but there is another form of suffering that is not found in a lack of meaning, *but in giving birth to new meaning*. It is a suffering that absorbs evil, freely and willingly, making of it an opportunity for a gift of forgiveness and compassion for the sinner, who in the end is not just damaging the victims of sin, but mutilating the sinner's own humanity. Such a willingness to suffer can both expose evil for what it really is in all its banality and disarm it of its power over us. For the power of evil lies in its ability to evoke like for like, to respond to evil with further evil, an eye for an eye or worse, and so there builds a spiral of violence and evil spinning out of control, destroying all who cross its path. Forgiveness and compassion break this spiraling of evil. Indeed, this power to undo the spiral of violence and evil is evident, not just at an individual

---

16. Ironically, this stance seems to be taken by some in the atheist movement, for whom religion is the source of all evil and must be eradicated.
17. Here I agree with the basic insight of Kenneth Surin, in *Theology and the Problem of Evil* (Oxford: Blackwell, 1986), that evil fundamentally is a practical and not a theoretical problem, though I do not adopt his complete theological agenda.

level, but communally and historically, as witnessed in the process of truth and reconciliation in South Africa.[18]

What would it mean for God to implement a divinely originated solution to the problem of evil? Such a solution might provide us with resources that were otherwise not available to us in this process of turning evil around into an opportunity for good. It might provide us with an inner assurance that we are loved and valuable to God, whatever the impositions of evil upon us. Without such an assurance, suffering in the face of evil can become a form of masochism or self-loathing. The solution might not just allow us to passively endure the imposition of evil upon us; it might empower us to actively confront evil in all its manifestations. We might be emboldened to stand up for the cause of ourselves and others for whom justice has been denied. This empowerment might then become socially and culturally transformative, not just over decades but over centuries or millennia. As a social reality, the solution might become embodied in a tradition that promotes belief in God and in God's solution to the problem of evil, in our accountability to God for our actions, as well as spiritual practices that strengthen us in the moral challenges we face in a world where the reign of sin—wars, crime, drug addiction and the drug trade, sexual violence, political corruption, environmental degradation, and so on—often seems to have the upper hand.

In the face of this struggle, the solution might also provide us with a hope that goes beyond mere human optimism that things will get better in the long run, but is grounded in the fact that God has chosen this creation from among all possible creations, and as such evil will never have the last word. In the end, however mysteriously, God will

---

18. For a fuller account of the social and cultural dimensions of the solution to the problem of evil, see Neil Ormerod, *Creation, Grace and Redemption* (Maryknoll, NY: Orbis, 2007), 153–73.

turn the situation around. This is not a counsel to do nothing, but an antidote to despair when all other hope is exhausted.

If such a social solution exists, we would expect it to place a high priority on the importance of forgiveness and compassion. These are the values that a redemptive suffering gives birth to, not as an abstraction, but as forgiveness of and compassion for this person who has done me wrong. This is not an offer of cheap grace that dismisses the importance of the offense; rather, it is a facing of the reality of the evil that has been done in all its dimensions while still being able to offer forgiveness and to feel compassion for a fellow human being who has become trapped in cycles of self-destruction.

Such a community would also embody forgiveness and compassion toward me when I fail, as almost inevitably I will, in dealing with the moral struggles of human existence. We would expect it also to place a high priority on love, to seek to build up communities of love that teach us that we are truly loved and lovable and encourage us to love others in our turn as well. Then we can face the challenges of turning the other cheek, of praying for those who persecute us, and of going the extra mile in the struggle against evil.

Finally, there is the possibility of a most radical form of the solution to the problem of evil, where God enters into our human condition to manifest the divinely originated solution to the problem of evil "from the inside." Such an entry would not be on a par with ancient myths of gods taking human form while fully maintaining all their divine powers, but rather a genuine entry into the human condition with all its limitations and sufferings, being tempted in every way that we are, but living a life that fully manifests love, compassion, and forgiveness through redemptive suffering.

I could push the analysis further, but the reader may complain that my biases as a Christian theologian are becoming too evident.[19] The discussion above remains hypothetical in the sense that it asks how we might address the problem of evil and how God might manifest a solution to the problem of evil. As such, it pertains to the task of a natural theology, as affirming God's existence and acknowledging the problem of evil, but then pushes the issue further by asking what God might be doing about the problem of evil. Asking whether and in what ways such a solution might actually be implemented would move us beyond the realm of natural theology and into a comparative study of how religions address the problem of evil. This lies beyond the scope of the present work.

To sum up, any solution to the problem of evil cannot detract from the imperatives to be intelligent, reasonable, and responsible. Any solution must rather enhance and reinforce these imperatives, because the problem of evil lies precisely in our failure to adhere to them. It must be in an intelligible continuity with the created order, not an alien imposition upon it. It must meet the requirements of reason, not as a logical deduction from premises, but as providing sound evidence of its fruitfulness; and it must call us to a greater responsibility to face the depths of the problem of evil and accept a responsibility to turn evil into an opportunity for good.

Conclusion

This work began with a discussion of the place and nature of natural theology, arguing that a contemporary natural theology should aspire to be contextual, public, and political in its range. As contextual, it seeks to respond to the claims of the new atheists that science renders belief in God unnecessary and can on its own explain the origins

---

19. As a Christian theologian, I believe that the Christian tradition manifests in history the divinely originated solution to the problem of evil. However, I also recognize that at times non-Christians have been exemplary in manifesting this same solution. For example, the nonviolent active resistance to evil practiced by Mohandas Ghandi, particularly his experiments with truth, are in conformity with what I have outlined above.

of the universe and of human morality. These claims have been shown to be specious. In fact, the scientific method presumes the intelligibility of the universe and accepts as a matter of brute fact its contingency. Both these matters lie beyond the scope of the scientific method to resolve, and both point to a source of intelligibility and existence that transcends this universe. The claim that morality is reducible to biology is inconsistent with the performance of the chief proponent of that claim, Richard Dawkins, who has an implicit nonbiological moral teleology operative in his stated agenda, "If this book works as I intend, the religious readers who open it will be atheists when they put it down."[20]

This work has also taken up the question of the political implications of a publicly asserted natural theology as a way of addressing concerns that the public acknowledgment of God's existence leads inevitably to a theocratic state. In making these arguments, while I have drawn from various Christian authors (as well as pre-Christian philosophical authors), I have not done so in a way that claims them as authoritative sources, but as illustrative of the type of argument being deployed. Nothing in this work has claimed the authority of a religious tradition, and so it is a form of public theology.

Nonetheless, as a culture we are far from promoting a community of metaphysicians who would have the requisite intellectual and moral orientations to make a natural theology a sustainable enterprise. The major issue here is that of what Lonergan has called "intellectual conversion." This conversion is not an alien imposition onto science, but rather asks that the basic criteria of a scientist's knowing be aligned with her criteria of what is real. As knowing is a matter of intelligence and reason, reality becomes what is known

20. Dawkins, *The God Delusion*, 5.

through intelligence and reason, not by taking a good look. However, the myth of reality as "already-out-there-now" is deeply embedded in our culture, even among those who would claim to be metaphysicians. It drives a materialistic reductionism that is simply not required by, or in the end congruent with, scientific method. It proclaims as unreal our whole world of meanings and values, and dismisses the inner life of consciousness that generates that world of meanings and values as merely "epiphenomenal." It is a bleak vision of reality, a vision of a universe without meaning, purpose, or hope, and we need to be saved from it. One wonders why some find it so attractive. However, with intellectual conversion we can break the myth of the real as already-out-there-now and begin to recover not only the full reality of all the sciences (as not just subdivisions of particle physics), but also the full reality of our human world of meanings and values and the inner life that generates and sustains them.

Intellectual conversion allows us to recognize the full reality of human values, which then also raises the question of moral conversion. Are there moral requirements that are imposed upon us, not as a matter of choice, but as given elements of our existence? Is the world of values something each of us decides for ourselves, or it is in some sense "objective" not as an already-out-there-now real but as something we can intelligently grasp and reasonably affirm? If this is so, then moral conversion implies conforming ourselves to this preexisting moral universe, whose contours we must nonetheless learn to uncover and appreciate. This moral universe, which is the universe of being, is also a created contingent order, created by a God who is the author and sustainer of the moral order, the one to whom we are ultimately accountable.

Finally, both intellectual and moral conversion allow us to address the classical questions of theodicy: why the universe contains pain, suffering, and evil. Indeed, even in the making of such distinctions, these conversions are helpful. While not claiming to be the final word on the topic, it does delineate the issues related particularly to the problem of evil and how this problem is to be addressed as a practical problem. Indeed, I have gone so far as to suggest the outlines of a divinely originated solution to the problem of evil, leaving to the reader to inquire as to whether there is evidence of such a solution present in human history.

Bibliography

Aristotle. *The Basic Works of Aristotle*. Edited by Richard McKeon. Modern Library Classics. New York: Random House, 2009.

Augustine. *The Confessions*. Translated by Maria Boulding. New York: Vintage Books, 1998.

———. *The Trinity*. Translated by Edmund Hill. Edited by John E. Rotelle, OSA. Brooklyn, NY: New City, 1991.

Barrow, John D, and Frank J. Tipler. *The Anthropic Cosmological Principle*. Oxford: Oxford University Press, 1988.

Beards, Andrew. *Method in Metaphysics: Lonergan and the Future of Analytic Philosophy*. Toronto: University of Toronto Press, 2008.

The Blackwell Companion to Natural Theology. Edited by William Lane Craig and J. P. Moreland. Oxford: Blackwell, 2009.

Bokenkotter, Thomas S. *A Concise History of the Catholic Church*. Rev. and expanded ed. New York: Doubleday, 2004.

Boyarin, Daniel. "Semantic Differences; or 'Judaism'/'Christianity'." In *The Ways That Never Parted: Jews and Christians in Late Antiquity and the Early Middle Ages*, edited by Adam H. Becker and Annette Yoshiko Reed, 65–85. Tübingen: Mohr Siebeck, 2003.

Burgess, John, and Gideon Rosen. *A Subject with No Object*. Oxford: Oxford University Press, 1997.

Davies, Paul. *The Goldilocks Enigma: Why Is the Universe Just Right for Life?* London: Allen Lane, 2006.

Dawkins, Richard. *The God Delusion*. London: Bantam, 2006.

———. *The Selfish Gene*. 30th anniversary ed. Oxford/New York: Oxford University Press, 2006.

Dobell, Brian. *Augustine's Intellectual Conversion: The Journey from Platonism to Christianity*. Cambridge: Cambridge University Press, 2009.

Doran, Robert M. *Theology and the Dialectics of History*. Toronto: University of Toronto Press, 1990.

Feyerabend, Paul. *Against Method*. Edited by Bert Terpstra. Chicago: University of Chicago Press, 1999.

Flew, Antony, and Roy Abraham Varghese. *There Is a God: How the World's Most Notorious Atheist Changed His Mind*. 1st ed. New York: HarperOne, 2007.

Gillespie, Michael Allen. *The Theological Origins of Modernity*. Chicago: University of Chicago Press, 2008.

Girard, René, Jean-Michel Oughourlian, and Guy Lefort. *Things Hidden since the Foundation of the World*. Stanford, CA: Stanford University Press, 1987.

Goetz, Stewart. "The Argument from Evil." In *The Blackwell Companion to Natural Theology*, edited by William Lane Craig and J. P. Moreland, 449–97. Oxford: Blackwell, 2009.

Greene, Brian. *The Elegant Universe: Superstrings, Hidden Dimensions, and the Quest for the Ultimate Theory*. London: Jonathan Cape, 1999.

Hart, Kevin. *The Trespass of the Sign: Deconstruction, Theology, and Philosophy*. 2nd ed. Perspectives in Continental Philosophy. New York: Fordham University Press, 2000.

Hawking, Stephen. "Black Hole Explosions?" *Nature* 248 (March 1, 1974): 30–31.

Hick, John. *Evil and the God of Love*. London: Macmillan, 1966.

Hitchens, Christopher. *God Is Not Great: How Religion Poisons Everything.* 1st ed. New York: Twelve, 2007.

Jaspers, Karl. *The Origin and Goal of History.* New Haven, CT: Yale University Press, 1953.

Kanigel, Robert. *The Man Who Knew Infinity: A Life of the Genius Ramanujan.* New York: Washington Square, 1992.

Kant, Immanuel. *Religion within the Boundaries of Mere Reason and Other Writings.* Edited by Allen Wood, George Di Giovanni, and Robert Merrihew Adams. Cambridge Texts in the History of Philosophy. Cambridge/New York: Cambridge University Press, 1998.

Kelly, Anthony. *Eschatology and Hope.* Theology in Global Perspective. Maryknoll, NY: Orbis, 2006.

Kerr, Fergus. "Knowing God by Reason Alone: What Vatican I Never Said." *New Blackfriars* 91, no. 1033 (2010): 215–28.

Koestler, Arthur. *The Act of Creation.* London: Hutchinson, 1976.

Krauss, Lawrence. *A Universe from Nothing: Why There Is Something Rather Than Nothing.* New York: Free Press, 2012.

———. *The Physics of Star Trek.* New York: Basic Books, 1995.

Kritsky, G. "Darwin's Madagascan Hawk Moth Prediction." *American Entomologist* 37 (2001): 206–10.

Kuhn, Thomas S. *The Structure of Scientific Revolutions.* 2nd ed. Chicago: University of Chicago Press, 1970.

Küng, Hans. *Does God Exist? An Answer for Today.* Garden City, NY: Doubleday, 1980.

Leithart, Peter J. *Defending Constantine: The Twilight of an Empire and the Dawn of Christendom.* Downers Grove, IL: IVP Academic, 2010.

Lewis, C. S. *The Great Divorce.* New York: HarperCollins, 2001.

———. *The Problem of Pain.* New York: HarperOne, 2001.

Lindsay, Mark R. *Barth, Israel, and Jesus: Karl Barth's Theology of Israel.* Barth Studies. Hampshire: Ashgate, 2007.

Lonergan, Bernard J. F. "The Absence of God in Modern Culture." In *A Second Collection*, edited by William Ryan and Bernard Tyrell, 101–16. Philadelphia: Westminster, 1974.

———. "The General Character of the Natural Theology of Insight." In *Philosophical and Theological Papers 1965–1980*, edited by Robert M. Doran and Frederick E. Crowe, 3–9. Toronto: University of Toronto Press, 2004.

———. *Insight: A Study of Human Understanding*. Edited by Frederick E. Crowe and Robert M. Doran. Collected Works of Bernard Lonergan 3. Toronto: University of Toronto Press, 1992.

———. *Method in Theology*. London: DLT, 1972.

———. "Natural Knowledge of God." In *A Second Collection*, edited by William Ryan and Bernard Tyrrell, 117–33. Philadelphia: Westminster Press, 1974.

Loux, M. J., and D. W. Zimmerman, eds. *The Oxford Handbook of Metaphysics*. Oxford/New York: Oxford University Press, 2003.

MacIntyre, Alasdair. *After Virtue: A Study in Moral Theory*. 2nd ed. Notre Dame, IN: University of Notre Dame Press, 1984.

———. *Whose Justice? Which Rationality?* Notre Dame, IN: University of Notre Dame Press, 1988.

Maudlin, Tim. "Distilling Metaphysics from Quantum Mechanics." In *The Oxford Handbook of Metaphysics*, edited by M. J. Loux and D.W. Zimmerman, 461–90. Oxford/New York: Oxford University Press, 2003.

McGrath, Alister E. *Dawkins' God: Genes, Memes, and the Meaning of Life*. Malden, MA: Blackwell, 2005.

———. *A Fine-Tuned Universe: The Quest for God in Science and Theology*. 1st ed. Louisville: Westminster John Knox, 2009.

———. *The Open Secret: A New Vision for Natural Theology*. Malden, MA: Blackwell, 2008.

————. *Why God Won't Go Away: Is the New Atheism Running on Empty?* Nashville: Thomas Nelson, 2010.

McGrath, Alister E, and Joanna McGrath. *The Dawkins Delusion: Atheist Fundamentalism and the Denial of the Divine.* Downers Grove, IL: InterVarsity, 2007.

Moore, Andrew. "Should Christians Do Natural Theology?" *Scottish Journal of Theology* 63 (2010): 127–45.

Moreland, J. P. "The Argument from Consciousness." In *The Blackwell Companion to Natural Theology,* edited by William Lane Craig and J. P. Moreland, 282–343. Oxford: Blackwell, 2009.

Newman, John Henry. *An Essay in Aid of a Grammar of Assent.* London: Burns, Oates and Co., 1874.

Novak, Michael. *Will It Liberate? Questions About Liberation Theology.* New York: Paulist Press, 1986.

O'Malley, John W. *What Happened at Vatican II.* Cambridge, MA: Belknap, 2008.

Oerter, Robert. *The Theory of Almost Everything: The Standard Model, the Unsung Triumph of Modern Physics.* New York: Penguin Group, 2006.

Ormerod, Neil. "Charles Taylor and Bernard Lonergan on Natural Theology." *Irish Theological Quarterly* 74 (2009): 419–33.

————. *Creation, Grace and Redemption.* Maryknoll, NY: Orbis, 2007.

————. "God and Politics." *Australasian Catholic Record* 84 (2007): 3–10.

————. "In Defence of Natural Theology: Bringing God into the Public Realm." *Irish Theological Quarterly* 71 (2007): 227–41.

————. "Preliminary Steps Towards a Natural Theology." *Irish Theological Quarterly* 76 (2011): 115–27.

————. "Secularisation and the 'Rise' of Atheism." *Australian EJournal of Theology* 17 (2010): 13–22.

Ormerod, Neil, and Cynthia S. W. Crysdale. *Creator God, Evolving World.* Minneapolis: Fortress Press, 2013.

Plantinga, Alvin, and James F. Sennett. *The Analytic Theist: An Alvin Plantinga Reader*. Grand Rapids: Eerdmans, 1998.

Popper, Karl R. *Conjectures and Refutations: The Growth of Scientific Knowledge*. New York: Basic Books, 1962.

Rees, Martin J. *Just Six Numbers: The Deep Forces That Shape the Universe*. New York: Basic Books, 2000.

Singh, Simon. *Fermat's Last Theorem: The Story of a Riddle That Confounded the World's Greatest Minds for 358 Years*. London: Fourth Estate, 1998.

Spitzer, Robert J. *New Proofs for the Existence of God: Contributions of Contemporary Physics and Philosophy*. Grand Rapids: Eerdmans, 2010.

Surin, Kenneth. *Theology and the Problem of Evil*. Oxford: Blackwell, 1986.

Swinburne, Richard. *The Existence of God*. Oxford/New York: Oxford University Press, 1979.

Tanner, Kathryn. *God and Creation in Christian Theology: Tyranny and Empowerment?* Minneapolis: Fortress Press, 2004.

———. *Theories of Culture: A New Agenda for Theology*. Minneapolis: Fortress Press, 1997.

Taylor, Charles. *A Secular Age*. Cambridge, MA: Belknap, 2007.

———. *Sources of the Self: The Making of the Modern Identity*. Cambridge, MA: Harvard University Press, 1989.

Thomson, John A. F. *The Western Church in the Middle Ages*. London: Arnold, 1998.

Tyrrell, Bernard. *Bernard Lonergan's Philosophy of God*. Notre Dame, IN: University of Notre Dame Press, 1974.

Voegelin, Eric. *The New Science of Politics: An Introduction*. Chicago: University of Chicago Press, 1952.

———. "The Philosophy of Existence: Plato's 'Gorgias'." *The Review of Politics* 11/4 (1949): 477–98.

Whitehead, Alfred North, and Bertrand Russell. *Principia Mathematica*. Cambridge: Cambridge University Press, 1910.

Zerjal, Tatiana, Yali Xue, Giorgio Bertorelle, R. Spencer Wells, Weidong Bao, Suling Zhu, Raheel Qamar, Qasim Ayub, Aisha Mohyuddin, Songbin Fu, Pu Li, Nadira Yuldasheva, Ruslan Ruzibakiev, Jiujin Xu, Qunfang Shu, Ruofu Du, Huanming Yang, Matthew E. Hurles, Elizabeth Robinson, Tudevdagva Gerelsaikhan, Bumbein Dashnyam, S. Qasim Mehdi, and Chris Tyler-Smith. "The Genetic Legacy of the Mongols." *American Journal of Human Genetics* 72/3 (2003): 717–21.

Index